Praise for *Win W*

'I have worked with Derek for 25 years; as a competitor and then as a provider of training to businesses for which I have had responsibility. His observations on behaviours and outcomes are perceptive: they encourage a different way of thinking and lead to much more effective outcomes.' *Steve Pateman, Head of UK Banking, Santander UK*

'I wish I could get all the lawyers in our worldwide practice to read this book.' *Peter Hirst, Senior Partner, Clyde & Co Lawyers*

'An expert's guide to a difficult business subject. All our MBA students have access to Derek's programme and all business leaders should read this.' *Professor Andy Adcroft, Leader, Surrey University Business School MBA programme*

'I have worked with Derek for almost 5 years and there's nothing he does not know about negotiation. This book should be on every CEO's bookshelf!' *Laura Sercombe, CEO, Challengers*

'For the past 30 years I have listened to many negotiation experts. Although many have great ideas and strategies, nobody has as much real-life, practical advice, based on real world experience as Derek Arden.' *Patricia Fripp, first female President of The National Speakers Association (USA)*

'Derek has incorporated all the gems of his excellent material on this vital subject into this book. A must for all negotiators, whatever their level of experience.' *Michael Williams, Chairman, Sovereign Business Integration Group Plc*

'In this book you will find all you need to know on negotiating the largest deals to the smallest transactions.' *Dr Nido Qubein, President of Highpoint University and Chairman, Great Harvest Bread Company*

'Everyone in business should read this book.' *Professor David Gray, University of Greenwich, London*

'The best book on negotiation I have ever read.' *Matt Tumbridge, CEO, Used Car Expert*

'There are skills in here that everyone should use.' *Graham Jones, Internet Psychologist*

Win Win

Win Win

How to get a winning result from persuasive negotiations

Derek Arden

Harlow, England • London • New York • Boston • San Francisco • Toronto • Sydney
Auckland • Singapore • Hong Kong • Tokyo • Seoul • Taipei • New Delhi
Cape Town • São Paulo • Mexico City • Madrid • Amsterdam • Munich • Paris • Milan

Pearson Education Limited
Edinburgh Gate
Harlow CM20 2JE
United Kingdom
Tel: +44 (0)1279 623623
Web: www.pearson.com/uk

First published 2015 (print and electronic)

ISBN: 978-1-292-07408-5 (print)
      978-1-292-07409-2 (PDF)
      978-1-292-07410-8 (eText)
      978-1-292-07411-5 (ePub)

British Library Cataloguing-in-Publication Data
A catalogue record for the print edition is available from the British Library

Library of Congress Cataloging-in-Publication Data
Arden, Derek.
  Win win : how to get a winning result from persuasive negotiations / Derek Arden.
    pages cm
  Includes index.
  ISBN 978-1-292-07408-5 (print) – ISBN 978-1-292-07409-2 (PDF) –
  ISBN 978-1-292-07410-8 (eText) – ISBN 978-1-292-07411-5 (ePub)
  1. Negotiation in business.   I. Title.
  HD58.6.A74 2015
  658.4'052--dc23

                                                  2015015701

10 9 8 7 6 5 4 3 2 1
19 18 17 16 15

Cover design: Two Associates

Print edition typeset in 9.5/12.5pt Scene Std by 35
Printed in Great Britain by Henry Ling Ltd, at the Dorset Press, Dorchester, Dorset

NOTE THAT ANY PAGE CROSS REFERENCES REFER TO THE PRINT EDITION

Contents

PART 3
HOTSPOTS

About the author

For over 25 years Derek Arden has been an international negotiator.

He first realised that there were vital negotiating skills to be learnt when he was asked to leave a meeting with the 3rd largest retailer in the world, after just 30 seconds, having refused to budge on the price of a £1 million contract.

That night, on his way home, he bought his first book on negotiating and, from then on, went on to study every meaningful book and audio set and watch every video published by the leading global experts on the subject.

Derek has lived the experiences, studied the experts, applied their principals and simplified their combined wisdom into a simple doable system.

He went to Harvard Business School to study under Professor Bill Ury, the acknowledged world expert on negotiations and co-author of *Getting to Yes: Negotiating an Agreement Without Giving In* (1991). He then studied psychology and the interaction between people and situations in which they find themselves. An avid people watcher, one of his first publications was on reading body language.

Whilst working in his full-time job, he was asked to speak at London and European Business Schools, due to his practical hands-on ability as a practising negotiator. He became a visiting lecturer at Henley Business School for 12 years and now teaches in MBA programmes at Surrey University.

After leaving full-time employment, he set up his own consultancy, the Negotiating Agency, and became a global speaker.

His techniques work universally because there is no jargon and they are exceptionally practical. As a result, Derek has been invited to speak to companies on all 5 continents and in 27 countries.

Derek has been passionate about making the art and science of negotiating practical and hands-on, with an honest, simple and non-jargon approach.

When Pearson was looking for an author for its 2015 book, it scoured the globe for the right information and the right author, and discovered Derek's work. Pearson approached Derek to write a book that could be published under its brand, meeting the wish of both of them for it to fulfil the criteria of being practical, easy to read and win win.

Today, Derek's advice is in demand at the negotiating table, in the boardroom and on the convention stage.

Derek's qualifications include Chartered Fellow of the Institute of Financial Services, Fellow of the Chartered Management Institute and Fellow of the Professional Speaking Association. He also chairs the board of directors of the Professional Speaking Association. You can find out more from the following online resources:

www.derekarden.com
www.youtube.com/derekarden
www.twitter.com/derekarden

Author's acknowledgements

Thank you to Sally, Mark, Jenny, Enid and Stan for your encouragement, understanding and wisdom; without which this book would not have been possible.

In addition I would like to thank all my friends, colleagues and business associates for all their advice, inspiration and stories.

There are too many to name here.

Publisher's acknowledgements

The publisher would like to thank the following for their kind permission to reproduce their photographs:

Pearson Education Ltd: Sven Hoppe, p. 247; **Professor Peter Thompson**: p. 115, Source: Thompson, P., Margaret Thatcher: A New Illusion, *Perception*, 1980, 9, 483–4.

All other images © Pearson Education

QR Code is a registered trademark of DENSO WAVE INCORPORATED.

Every effort has been made to trace the copyright holders and we apologise in advance for any unintentional omissions. We would be pleased to insert the appropriate acknowledgement in any subsequent edition of this publication.

Foreword

It is a privilege to write the foreword to this outstanding book.

I have known Derek Arden for over 25 years in both a business and a personal capacity.

He has always had an insatiable appetite to help people learn. In fact, the key reason he left his very senior job in financial services was because he wanted to pursue an educational career rather than one in the 24/7 world of the global financial sector in London.

We first met across the negotiating table when he worked for one part of a global financial services firm and I worked in another area. Some of the internal negotiations were as difficult as the external ones, if not more so. They often can be!

As Derek says, all the issues we face as we go through the journey of life, in the cut and thrust of the speed of change, are negotiations.

I like Derek; I like his honesty, his common sense and his motivation to make every effort to achieve a negotiated win win situation.

I commend you to read this book from cover to cover several times. Dip in and out of it, as it contains every aspect of business negotiating skills that you will ever need.

There not much that Derek Arden does not know about the psychology of negotiating, selling and influencing. Use this book to enhance your results, your career and your business. This is a critical top priority success factor.

Justin Urquart Stewart

Justin Urquhart Stewart is one of the most recognisable and trusted market commentators on television, radio and in the press. Originally trained as a lawyer, he has observed the retail market industry for 30 years whilst in corporate banking and stockbroking, and has developed a unique understanding of the market's roles and benefits for the private investor.

Introduction

This book is written to encompass all the practical areas I have learnt over 25 years:

1. as an international business negotiator
2. as a student of the best academic negotiating brains on the planet (at Harvard Business School and their negotiation project)
3. as a professional speaker who has made every attempt to explain these concepts in simple terms from the stage in 27 countries and on all 5 continents.

I have kept it simple and easy to read. It is divided into three easily accessible parts. At each stage, I have applied the KISS rule – keep it short and simple – easy to read, digest and implement.

The parts

Part 1 is about negotiation and why you, the reader, should be negotiating all the time. Always looking at how to upgrade your skills. After all, negotiating encompasses every area of interpersonal skills. The more we learn, the more we earn – as one of my mentors once said.

Part 2 contains the 11 steps you need to know to be an effective negotiator and it gives you all the tips and techniques needed to continue to upgrade your skills in order to be a really excellent negotiator.

Part 3 has short chapters called *hotspots*. These are for referring to, as and when, for particular situations.

You can read the parts when you want to, or read them from beginning to end.

Each chapter starts with an outline of what you will learn and ends with a recap.

I have also included T!P TOP TIPS! throughout the book, as well as some appropriate warnings, to enable you to dip in and out of the book for any important negotiation you might have.

In addition, there is a self-assessment exercise for you to complete, which I hope you will find very useful.

There are so many stories I wanted to tell you to illustrate points – being asked to leave meetings in an aggressive way; being threatened, bugged; an attempt at being bribed; working with a prince – but I cannot, because of the confidential nature of the work I do.

In fact, my brilliant editor, Eloise Cook at Pearson, said to me once, and she does not mince her words, 'Derek, this story sounds more like an Andy McNab story than a business negotiation.' This was when we were set up in a room in Paris where we had every reason to believe the room had been bugged with listening devices. If you want to find out more about this story, why not get in touch?

I have made it my business over the last 25 years to ensure that I have always mixed with the highest achievers as, not only do you learn from them, their style and their substance rubs off. If you cannot meet them, then buy their books, go to their conventions and watch their videos. I have made every attempt to inject their wisdom into this book.

Underlying negotiation are psychological principles. The psychology of how people behave. Bear this in mind as you go through this book. What's in it for the other person? WII FM – not WII FM the radio station – but 'What's in it for me?'. Remember, everybody is different, and you never know where the other person is coming from until you ask!

Keep this book on your desk or in your library and refer to it whenever you are in a negotiating situation – which will be more often than you think. As a friend reminded me many years ago, self-development books are for using, not looking good on shelves: 'Self-development not shelf development'.

I wish you fantastic negotiations as you develop your skills. Remember:

1. Always leave some meat on the bone for the other side.
2. No matter how thin you slice it, there are two sides to everything.
3. Fail to prepare – prepare to fail.

I have made available online resources for you at www.derekarden.com – you will find daily blog entries (almost 900 to date) designed to help you help yourself as you move forward in this key life and business skill.

www.derekarden.co.uk/blog
www.twitter.com/derekarden

Use this QR code to access some more Tip Top Tips from Derek. Just download any free QR scanner app onto your smartphone or tablet from your app store. Then scan the code by pointing the camera of your device towards the code. It will read the code and take you to the web page linked to the code.

Alternatively go to: www.derekarden.co.uk/tip-top-tips/

Derek issues an Executive Briefing with 20 issues a year full of negotiating tips. This is free to people who have seen him speak or who have purchased this book. Send him an email at action@derekarden.co.uk to sign up to receive it.

Additionally Derek regularly interviews high achievers. To download the interviews go to: www.derekarden.co.uk/radio-podcasts/

PART 1
WHY NEGOTIATION MATTERS

1.
We are all negotiators

In this chapter you will learn:

- Negotiations happen 24/7/365. Any interaction with another person is a potential negotiation.
- We are born to be negotiators. Children know how to negotiate with their parents and no one taught them.
- Even when you are in a job. You are selling your time and expertise for a monetary return. Make sure you get paid what you are worth; you work for Me plc.

Introduction

I am always amazed when I speak at conferences on negotiating. I look at the audience and ask a very simple question: 'How many of you are negotiators?'

I get very few hands up. I get just a few nods. Of course, the real answer is that we are all negotiators. We negotiate all the time. Whether it is with our children, our partner, our spouse, our business colleagues, our clients or even ourselves.

Of course, it does depend on the audience of where I am speaking. With a business audience I will get more hands up than I would do with a more general audience. I am always surprised that many people do not think of themselves as negotiators. Nor do they think that they are negotiating so many times during the day. It is an eye opener and I hope this book will be an eye opener for you.

Negotiating with yourself

I always say the first negotiation is with yourself. Why do I say that? Because, generally, it is easier not to negotiate than negotiate. As you read this book, you will appreciate more and more the psychology of the negotiating process.

The fact is that negotiating takes a little thinking time on the best way to approach the issue and sometimes it will produce some conflict. The way you approach that conflict, perhaps in a soft non-threatening way, will directly affect the outcome.

So, your own mindset, your own psychological state and your approach to how you negotiate, will affect you and the outcome.

Let's face it – successful people in business and in life are successful negotiators. They have to be and it has either been self-taught or learnt from others, from books like this, workshops, seminars and masterclasses.

Where are you as a negotiator on a scale of 0–100?

I also ask this question at the beginning of my masterclasses. I am asking you, at the beginning of this book, to consider the question.

Generally, the majority of participants score themselves somewhere between 40 and 70. That is 80 per cent of people. The other 20 per cent are either below, between 20 and 40, or above 70 but not much above 80.

The next question to ask yourself is – how good is good enough as a negotiator?

If you have scored yourself 60 – what would it take to be a 70? And then to move up to an 80 or even a 90? What difference would that make? Would that be the difference that makes the difference to your business, your relationships and your life?

> **T!P TOP TIP!**
> Ask yourself – what is the difference that makes the difference when you are negotiating?

Negotiation is a 24/7/365 skill

Every human interaction is a negotiation and we learn to be good at it early on, as a child. In fact, almost as soon as we are born, we cry and find that crying gets us fed.

If you asked a behavioural psychologist what that does to us, they would say that the response becomes an anchor, a Pavlovian response: make a fuss and you get attention.

Of course, as we grow up, we learn that there are better ways of getting what we want. Although often I come across people who negotiate emotionally; throwing their toys out of the pram, metaphorically speaking.

Almost every area in your life, almost every moment of your life when you have interactions with others, is a negotiating situation.

Dale Carnegie wrote one of the first, and still one of the best, interpersonal skills books over 70 years ago, with the great title, How to Win Friends and Influence People. It has been reprinted many times. In essence, it says if you help people get what they want, they will help you get what you want.

> **TIP TOP TIP!**
> If you help others get what they want, then they will help you get what you want – sometimes called the Law of Reciprocity (see Chapter 14).

Ages of negotiators

I once read that the best ages for negotiating are 0–16 and 32–50.

Up to 16 we are pretty uninhibited. This seems to make sense to me in what I have observed. Before our teens we push the boundaries of discovery. In our teens we can be pretty awkward, as we prepare to leave the nest and find out as much as we can about life. So, in those years, we are pretty much in it for ourselves, pushing our luck as much as we can.

Around 16 we become more aware of what is going on around us, and stop asking.

Asking is one of the most important skills in negotiating. Asking great questions and listening carefully.

With the stopping of asking as we mature, and as we respect other people more, comes the embarrassment of asking in negotiation scenarios.

At about 32 people who are moderately to seriously ambitious start taking more serious responsibilities in business and realise that they have to go for it.

They get stuck in, negotiate and show what they can do.

At around 50 they ease off, as they might prefer quicker deals, with less emphasis on the smaller detail.

I have found this is generally true, particularly with teenagers, as they are pushing the boundaries with their parents.

Life is a choice

It is our life and we can choose whether to get the maximum out of it or not.

There are always choices, although some people prefer not to give it much thought and just hope for the best.

I remember a friend of mine called Mike who said, 'I am stuck in a job going nowhere, a job with no prospects and I have a large mortgage.'

Mike had a choice. He could continue to do nothing and feel sorry for himself or decide to take action and sort himself and his life out.

The vast majority of people decide to take the passive route of doing nothing and wonder why it is nothing that they end up with.

In Mike's case, he had to give up certain things in order to gain others. Whilst we live in an abundant universe, there are some things that are finite.

The main finite thing we all have is the amount of time we have. We all have the same amount of hours in a day, minutes in an hour and seconds in a minute.

It is about energy management. Managing your energy and your motivation. Motivation is helped by setting yourself targets.

There are 24 hours in a day, during which the average person sleeps for 7.5 hours, travels for 2 hours, eats for 1.5 hours and works for 8 hours. This leaves 5 hours spare for other interests, which is a massive 35 hours a week.

You have lots of time to take forward your life in a different direction.

So, Mike sat down and thought about where he wanted to be in all aspects of his life. He then imagined he had done it, eight years down the track.

He visualised what he looked like, how he felt, what sounds he was hearing in his head and how people perceived him. He felt good.

Having drawn up his plan, he started taking action.

His life changed, he started negotiating with himself and with others and he is now very successful.

Take action, start negotiating.

The first negotiation is with you, and this is in your mind. We have a choice: to look at issues in life as a negotiation. The choice, then, is either to negotiate or take things as they are given to us.

> **T!P TOP TIP!**
> It is what you learn when you think you know it all that really counts.

Me plc

It is often said that we work for Me plc. Whoever employs us, we sell our time, our expertise and our services to them for a fee, a salary or a wage.

We get paid what the boss thinks is the rate for the job or we get paid the rate we negotiate! We can benchmark this against other people, other jobs and make sure we are being paid properly. We take into account the extras like health insurance, holidays, study leave, sick leave, etc.

Develop a mindset always to negotiate.

Everything is a negotiating situation.

WII FM

Finally, it is worth remembering what WII FM stands for. It is not a radio station; it stands for 'What's in it for me?'

What's in it for me? You will know what is in it for you. But, when you can understand what is in it for the other person, you can negotiate a truly win win win, whenever possible.

You are the most important person in the world. Until you look after you, you cannot help others. That is why, when you get on an aeroplane, they tell you to put your own oxygen mask on first before you help others.

In summary, negotiation is a life skill. An everyday skill and what I observe, as far as negotiating is concerned. Most people know what to do and then do not do what they know.

Recap

- The first negotiation is with yourself.

- You work for yourself, Me plc, so your negotiations directly or indirectly affect your income.

- Negotiating is a 24-hour skill.

- Remember WII FM: 'What's in it for me?'

- Keep your negotiating 'hat' on at all times.

2.
The cost of *not* negotiating

In this chapter you will learn:

- There is a huge unknown price to pay, if you do not negotiate.
- How to work out how much *not* negotiating 24/7 might cost you.
- There is a close correlation between how much you earn and your ability to negotiate.

Introduction

Some people like negotiating; and others do not.

Negotiating is all about being brave, being a little competitive and getting better deals.

I have travelled and spoken extensively all over the world and the following two facts I have found are interesting – if you will allow me to generalise a little.

1. There seem to be two types of people in the world:
   - people who *do* negotiate
   - people who *do not* negotiate.

2. And, coincidently, there are two prices in the world:
   - one price for people who *do not* negotiate
   - a second price for those who *do* negotiate.

What percentage of the population negotiates varies all over the world. This depends on cultures, traditions and the way people and regions have grown up.

The cost of not negotiating is hugely expensive!

Many businesses have got into serious trouble just because their negotiating skills were inadequate.

Can you afford not to be a professional negotiator?

My calculations

I have calculated that, since I started negotiating seriously over 25 years ago, I believe I have made or saved over £250,000 after I take into account compound interest.

If you made or saved just 10 per cent of that over the next 20 years of your life, then you would be £25,000 better off. And the portion that you saved on your costs would be tax free. It is money on which you have already paid tax.

On the next page is a calculator, the negotiation savings calculator (NSC). This is for you to work out how much you or your business might make or save.

Make the calculation

Get your pen out and do a quick calculation on how much you might make or save over the next 20 years if you negotiate seriously on everything.

You may be surprised how much extra money you might make – often more than most people have in their pension fund when they retire.

If you are employed, income will be increased pay, salary and bonuses, together with extras such as extra allowances, pension contributions and training days, etc.

If you work for yourself, income will be increased fees, prices and product sales.

Costs are costs. We should reduce our costs as much as we can. Shop around, price match, ask for lower prices.

WARNING!

Despite hard work – if you do not *negotiate*, you may not get what you deserve!

Additionally, if you do not ask, you do not give the other person the opportunity to say yes, which they may well be able to do!

If you do not ask, then the answer is automatically no to whatever you were thinking about asking for.

One of my clients, Alison, told me this is what she tells her three children. And now they ask for everything! She blames me; they are only four, six and eight.

You will see on the negotiation savings calculator that I have included a third category called soft pound deals, or bartering.

It is amazing how much you can save by using your skills to help others and in return they use their skills to help you, without any money changing hands.

Someone might fix my computer and I might give him or her some coaching on how to raise his or her fees.

Negotiating savings calculator (NSC)

Here is an explanation of how it works. Then you might like to consider what your own numbers are!

Tangible numbers

> *Line 1* – this line is either annual sales, if you are a business, or your various sources of annual income, if you are a private individual.

> Like most people, your only source of income might be your salary and bonus (if you are able to negotiate one). If so, it is important that you learn how to negotiate that area.

> *Line 2* – these are your costs – what you pay out each year, whether you are a business or not.

> If you are an individual, your costs are after tax, as tax is paid on your income. So any savings are, in effect, tax free!

Intangible items
I have not included these on the calculator but they have a benefit and a cost to you, depending how you handle them!

Swap deals – these are areas where you might swap what you do for what others can do for you. This requires a little outside-the-box thinking (see Chapter 10, Use your head). An example might be that you do someone's decorating (or something that you are good at and enjoy) and in return they give you lessons on the internet.

Relationships – wherever we have relationships there will always be varying degrees of disagreement and conflict. The ability to sort this out in a sensible win win win negotiated way can be extremely beneficial and cost efficient, whether it is with a business partner, a boss, your life partner, your spouse, a family member or your children. It is difficult to put a number in here but it is worth a little careful consideration as you learn to become an even better negotiator.

Figure 2.1 Negotiations savings calculator

> **Sales – income**
>   Increase by negotiation   =
>
> **Purchases – costs**
>   Decrease by negotiation   =
>
> *Total extra value per year, multiplied by number of years' savings, multiplied by compound investment rate over last period. (Over the last 100-year period the average return on stocks and shares and property investments has been over 12% pa.)*

Example 1 – Business

Year 1 – Extra sales and profit received due to negotiating	= £10,000
Extra cost savings by everyone negotiating	= £5,000
Total extra profit per year	£15,000
× the next 5 years for the business	= £75,000

Example 2 – Personal

Year 1 – Extra income/salary by negotiating

Increase by £1,000	=	£1,000
Cost savings by negotiating – £1,000	=	£1,000
Total	=	£2,000
× the next 20 years	=	£40,000

The *assumptions* here are for a business that does not have all its front-line people (front line: anyone in a selling, managerial or purchasing area) geared up to the premise 'Everything is negotiable' and they should be negotiating.

For an individual, it is for the majority of people who do not negotiate as a matter of course.

Savings are assumed over 20 years with no compounding of the savings. So, in theory, the increased profit/cash flow will be even better!

> **T!P TOP TIP!**
> Do not fight battles you cannot win. Sometimes, just agree, swallow your pride and move on.

Some interesting facts

Good negotiators earn more

> *While teaching, I have found a direct correlation between earnings and negotiating skills.*

I was privileged to be a visiting lecturer for over 12 years at the Henley Business School, whilst I was negotiating my way out of the financial services sector, before it all went pear shaped. At Henley they kept records, over a two-year period, of the people who attended the Strategic Management Course.

The course was for delegates, in senior management positions, from all over the world, who had been chosen to attend by their company because of their high potential.

The records related to how their line managers and peers rated certain skills. This was then compared with how much they earned. The typical manager attending was responsible for an average 231 people.

What the research showed was that a small number of delegates, 11 per cent, whose *salary was double* that of the average attendee, were rated by their manager as strongest in the following 5 competences, out of a total of 40:

- negotiating skills
- presentation skills
- oral expression – expressing yourself clearly
- appraisal of subordinates – picking the right people
- self-management – managing yourself and your work efficiently.

One of the benefits of using this book to increase your skills is that you are increasing your skills in one of the most important and effective subjects.

High achievers know how to get things done through people. They know how to get things from other people and they know how to make other people feel good.

I was speaking at a conference in Dunfermline, Scotland. I noticed a lady in the audience was giving me a particularly hard negative stare. Her body language was saying, 'There is no way I am going to negotiate.'

Afterwards, I spoke to the lady to see why she seemed so negative. I asked whether she enjoyed the conference and whether she would negotiate more. She responded that she felt very uncomfortable about negotiating. She felt negotiating price was particularly demeaning and people should always offer their best price; therefore negotiating should not be necessary.

This is a common problem for novice negotiators and, although it would be fantastic if we all offered our best prices, it is important to realise that there is a very hard side to business. Negotiating is extremely important, and helps to keep the other side honest. Help them keep their prices realistic.

If you feel uncomfortable or embarrassed about negotiating, then start small. Practise your negotiating skills, and build up to better things. Your skills and confidence will grow and so will the benefits.

And think back to the negotiation savings calculator – hasn't the amount you could have saved spurred you on to negotiate more?

Negotiation skills are highly desired in business

A 2013 survey by the Chartered Management Institute (CMI) showed that the most requested development priorities by line managers were:

1. Strategic decision making – 44 per cent
2. Negotiating and influencing – 35 per cent
3. Change management – 34 per cent
4. Coaching and mentoring – 33 per cent
5. Project management – 32 per cent

It found that, 'Negotiating training is what business managers wanted the most after strategic decision making.' Why?

Because the ability to negotiate well directly affects your results. There is no other skill that can make such a massive difference.

So, the CMI members wanted negotiating and influencing skills as their number two training priority in 2013, as they could see that it would be key to the businesses they worked in and their own success.

I therefore decided to turn my attention to the professions. I was speaking at a global convention of accountants in Sofia, Bulgaria, the 14th largest global accounting partnership in the world. I surveyed 91 of the attendees, all qualified in their profession:

1. 60 per cent of participants did not think they were good negotiators.
2. Only 21 per cent always haggled/bartered for goods and services.
3. Only 44 per cent said they recognised standard negotiating tactics when they were used on them.

4. Only 32 per cent said they recognised, read and interpreted body language – voice tonality meanings and language.

5. Only 46 per cent said they asked razor-sharp questions.

6. Finally, 32 per cent were not sure if they had told the truth. (This was the last question, as an experiment, to see how they responded.)

I asked psychologist Graham Jones to comment on these findings. He told me:

'As 32 per cent are not sure whether they have told the truth, they are reflecting on their gut instincts or perhaps lack of confidence in some of the areas you are questioning them on. Either way, it tells you that these people do not generally know about negotiation.

40 per cent say they are good negotiators (suggesting 60 per cent are not), yet only 21 per cent of them haggle. Only 44 per cent recognise negotiating tactics when they are used on them. Lots of room for improvement!'

You might notice that there are some inconsistences here, which is not unusual when you ask people about their negotiating acumen. Why? I believe negotiating skills are a bit like driving skills: most people are not going to admit they are not good as a negotiator, just as they would not admit to being a bad driver.

WARNING!

Just like a few things in life, *ego* takes over. Interestingly, the word *ego* is the 2nd, 3rd and 4th letter of the word negotiating. A good memory jogger: put your ego away when you are negotiating.

n**ego**tiating

Finally, a LinkedIn survey showed: More than one third of professionals are uncomfortable with presenting and negotiating.

Recap

- Do not forget the cost if you do not focus on pushing the envelope and negotiating at all times.

- Good negotiators are able to leverage their skills, the results they get and their own income.

- Negotiating is one of the key business skills and many professionals feel inadequate. So, by studying the subject, you will stand more chance of being even more successful.

- If you do not negotiate, someone else will get the benefits that you might get.

'The price of anything is the amount of life you exchange for it.'
HENRY THOREAU

3.
The *win win win* of negotiating

In this chapter you will learn:

- Negotiating is fundamental to your success in selling, influencing and handling difficult situations.

- A win win win situation is a win for me, a win for the other side and a win for the business relationship.

- When things get difficult, step aside from the issue for short while.

- To solve difficult negotiations, you sometimes need to be creative.

Introduction

The word negotiating sits in the middle of a number of disciplines.

Figure 3.1

Manipulating

Bullying

Harrassing

Presenting and pitching

Negotiating

Selling

Persuading

Influencing

These disciplines are important to get a successful negotiated outcome, negotiated deal or negotiated result. It does not matter what words we use – to be a good negotiator we have to be pretty good at:

- *Presenting and pitching* – to get us to the table.
- *Selling, persuading and influencing* – to get them to want to do the deal with us.
- *Questioning and listening* – to find out where they are coming from.
- *Haggling, bargaining and trading* – to get to the deal.

But there is also a darker side to negotiation – *manipulating, bullying and harassing*. You have to be on your guard for this, and be able to handle these effectively when they occur.

It is a mixed picture but, in the middle of all this, is negotiating. The better the negotiator, the better results you will get in all aspects of your life.

Negotiation is not just about you

Negotiation is central to everything we do in life and, like a lot of things, there are various outcomes.

When we have a discussion with someone and something is decided, that is the basic premise of any negotiation. Now you might think of that only in terms of who wins the negotiation – you or them. But, in fact, typically, there are four outcomes to a negotiation:

1. *Win/lose* – a win for you, a lose for them.
2. *Lose/win* – a lose for you, a win for them.
3. *Win/win* – a win for both of you.
4. *Lose/lose* – a lose for both of you.

Looking at the four outcomes above, probably you want the good result for you, but you should also think about good negotiation in terms of your ongoing relationship.

Figure 3.2

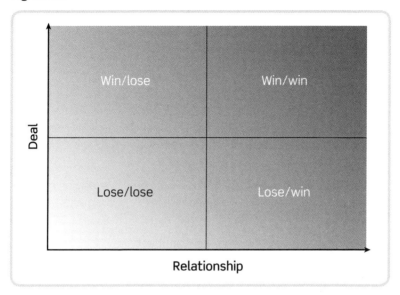

Chart these strategies graphically to see the outcome

In Figure 3.2, the vertical axis is the deal or the transaction and the horizontal axis is the ongoing relationship. A win win win is a win win with the promise of a real long-term relationship.

Rather than just thinking about the result you want, you should ensure the result of the negotiation is beneficial for both of you.

A win for you

A win for me

A win for both parties is a win win negotiation.

However, what if we take things one step further? Rather than just focusing on the result of this particular negotiation, you also need to bear in mind the needs of your ongoing relationship:

A win for you

A win for me

A win for us

A win for both parties and a win for the relationship is a win win win negotiation.

Win win win negotiations mean better negotiations, better relationships and better results.

T!P TOP TIP!

It is a general fact that it takes seven times more energy and time to attract a new customer than sell more to an existing customer *or* be introduced or referred by an existing customer to their contacts.

Therefore, *win win win* is a much more effective way of going about your negotiations in a positive sales environment.

Win win win negotiation can be the best way forward in this competitive, increasingly globally challenging and potentially dangerous world.

If you are not yet sure, try this game of noughts and crosses, as an introduction to win win win scenarios.

EXERCISE

Imagine you are playing a game of noughts and crosses with someone. Or, even better, find someone! Have a go – the objective is to score as many winning lines as possible.

Figure 3.3

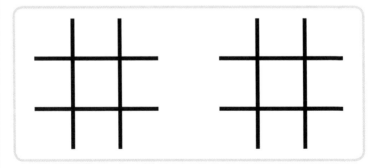

So, how did the two games go? Most people assume that the idea is to win as many lines as you can but to do that *they try to stop* the other person scoring winning lines of their own.

I have asked thousands of people across the world to play noughts and crosses and what normally happens in 91 per cent of games is that human competitiveness is switched on by the mere assumption that the objective is to get more for me and less for you to win. And this often happens in negotiations.

But think again: my instruction was that *'the objective of the game is to score as many winning lines as possible'*. It says nothing about stopping the other person scoring winning lines.

EXERCISE

Try the two games again. If you cooperate with your partner, then you have the opportunity to win eight lines each.

Figure 3.4

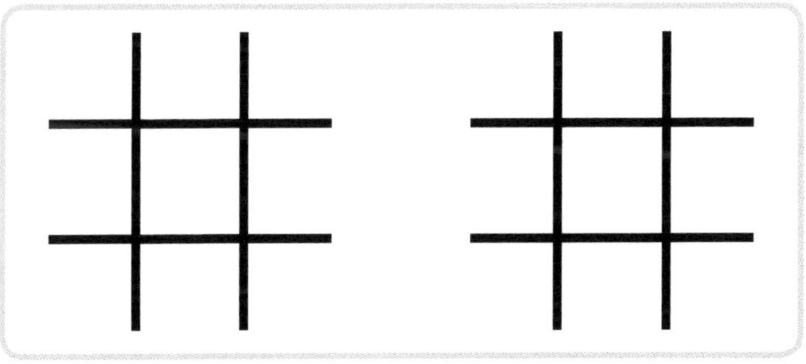

To get eight winning lines each, my crosses go on the top board and your noughts go on the bottom board, thereby achieving as much for me, and as much for you, by cooperation.

This is what your board should look like: a real win win win negotiation. You both get the result you want (you have each won a board) and you are both happy with the outcome.

Figure 3.5

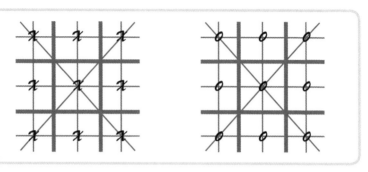

 WARNING!
There are people in life who just want to win, totally. The sooner you notice their behaviour, the quicker can you disengage from them.

You need to be careful if the person you are negotiating with does not care what happens to you, as long as they win. People who behave like this are not very nice to do business with. Perhaps you should move on as soon as you can.

The negotiating strategy you adopt should be linked directly to your business strategy with each individual customer. This will enable you to maximise your profit either on a long- or short-term basis.

Make sure your people know what your strategy is and act accordingly.

In a long-term partnership the synergistic benefits of a truly win win win situation cannot be overestimated.

Never forget that it is vital that all members of your team understand your strategy. If they do not, you risk not achieving your goals.

Here are three stories that illustrate the benefits of working towards the same goals.

1. THE PUSH BACK EXERCISE

This is an exercise that emphasises the benefits of win win and working together.

I first saw this at the Harvard Business School when I attended the 'Dealing with difficult people' workshop. The number one workshop in the world, they claimed at the time. I demonstrate this exercise often in masterclasses, as it makes a very valuable point. This was demonstrated by Professor William Ury, who co-wrote the ground-breaking book *Getting to Yes: Negotiating an Agreement Without Giving In* with Roger Fisher.

The professor asked one of the members of the seminar to come up and centre themselves (both feet planted firmly on the ground, the weight distributed evenly) with their palms outstretched.

He took the opposite position. (You could try it with a partner at some stage.)

As he leant and pushed against the person, the person pushed back in a competitive manner, which is the normal thing to do. The harder he pushed, the harder the other person pushed to maintain balance and not be pushed over.

This tends to happen in life: the harder someone pushes, the harder the other side pushes back, usually to the detriment of the situation, the outcome AND the deal.

Then Professor Ury did an unusual thing. He stopped pushing and moved to the side. The delegate had nothing to push against.

The energy of the resistance was not there. The person was pushing against air. The moral of the story is:

1. Sometimes we have to move to the side and stop pushing to see the big picture.

2. If we stop pushing back against the person, we can see the joint goal more clearly.

3. The person's argument collapsed when they thought about the consequences.

WARNING!

How hard are you pushing? Sometimes you should stand aside and reassess the situation. Let the right side of the brain think about the big picture and come up with alternatives.

2. THE PARABLE OF THE 17 CAMELS

There is a parable that goes back many thousands of years. See if you can work it out.

An old man dies, leaving three sons. His will says to give one half of his possessions to his eldest son, one third to his second-born son and one ninth to his youngest son. Not very fair, but that is what his wishes were.

Here is the problem. At the time of his death, he had 17 camels and no other possessions. The sons could not figure out how to divide the camels up, as the maths would not work.

While they were trying to think of a solution, a wise old woman came by and asked if she could help.

They told her the dilemma. She said maybe she could help by offering to give them one of her camels, as a gift.

This would mean that they had 18 camels. Now the maths works:

Half = 9

Third = 6

Ninth = 2

Problem solved.

However, the sons found that they had one camel left, so they gave the camel back to the wise old woman and they all went on their way.

The moral of the story is:

There is more than just one way to resolve a situation. Look for a win win win.

Note – this story is quoted many times in many different journals.

3. £20 GAME

There are a number of versions of this game, which make fantastic learning points to the negotiating bargaining process. They are good fun and illustrate the points we are making in this book.

Find two people and give them a £20 note or a similar note from the country you are in. Tell them – if you can negotiate a deal in 60 seconds on how to split the money between you, you can keep it. However, there are some rules:

> You cannot split it 50/50.
>
> If you cannot get to an agreement in one minute, you give the money back to me.

Reading this book, just stop and think for a minute what you might come up with. However, you might like to play this game with a couple of your team or business partners.

As you will have discovered, this needs a little creative thinking, which generally takes a bit of time.

People might come up with suggestions like:

1. It is better that one of us gets it rather than neither of us, so what about me taking it and I will buy the drinks the next time we meet.

2. Let's go £12/£8 and you will have £8 more than you would have had, if we do not agree.

3. I need the £20; I have a bill to pay this month. I will make it up to you when I see you next. Trust me.

When the time is up, it is likely that not only will you keep your £20, you can learn much about why negotiations often do not work.

The learning points here are similar to any negotiation. When time is short, people do not have time to stand back and have a think outside the box. You do not have time, you react, you do

➜

not think. When you do not have preparation time, you revert to looking after yourself.

So, how might we achieve a win win win here?

That is why we need variables, we need extras, we need to think about other things that we might want and what the other side might want.

Here are some creative solutions:

1. I take the £20, and I will wash your car, lend you my CDs, send you some eBooks.

2. I will post you a couple of good books I have finished with. I will send you Derek Arden's book *Presenting Phenomenally*.

3. I will give you a mentoring session on how to use LinkedIn.

4. I will show you how to use money-saving websites like Quidco.

Other solutions might be:

1. You take £10.01 and I will take £9.99. Some people are so competitive that they would want the extra penny just to prove a point.

2. Let me put in an extra £1. Now we are dividing £21 – you take £11 and I will take £10.

3. Let's split it £9 each. Now let's negotiate over the £2.

4. Toss a coin. If it is heads, you get £9 and I get £11. If it is tails, I get £11 and you get £9.

Most people do not reach these solutions. They do not see this as a partnership to work together. They see the other person as an opponent.

When we are short of time, when the WII FM factor comes in to play, most of the time people will try and make sure they win!

Recap

- Look for a win win win strategy when you negotiate.

- Remember, the two-board noughts and crosses scenario. Everybody wins.

- Stand aside to reassess any situation; it clarifies your thinking to return to joint goals where everyone wins.

- Remember to try and find the 18th camel.

4.
Rate your negotiation skills

In this chapter you will learn:

- How to use a self-assessment test to assess your negotiation skills. You will be able to take the test again at the end of the book to see how much you have improved.

Introduction

The score sheet (see Figure 4.1) is based on the chapters in Part 2 of this book, The 11 steps of negotiation. There is an opportunity for you to re-rate yourself after you have read the book and tried some of the skills. If you have not spent time preparing and studying the tools, techniques and tips in this book, it can be difficult to have confidence in a negotiation.

SELF-ASSESSMENT
1. Recall a recent negotiation and hold it in your mind.

2. Read through the questions below the score sheet. Then score yourself on your skills and ability in that negotiation. Give yourself a score out of 5 on the score sheet: 1 = low, 5 = excellent.

3. Multiply your score where indicated, then add up your total score. This will give you a score out of 100.

Figure 4.1 Score sheet

Your skills	Your rating	Multiplier	Your score
1 Prepare and plan	1 2 3 4 5	× 4	....
2 Give a great first impression	1 2 3 4 5	× 1	....
3 Ask the right questions	1 2 3 4 5	× 1	....
4 Listen well	1 2 3 4 5	× 2	....
5 Use your head	1 2 3 4 5	× 1	....
6 Read body language	1 2 3 4 5	× 2	....
7 Watch out for lying	1 2 3 4 5	× 1	....
8 Use the right strategies and tactics	1 2 3 4 5	× 3	....
9 Influence the other side	1 2 3 4 5	× 1	....
10 Know how to bargain	1 2 3 4 5	× 2	....
11 Know how to handle conflict	1 2 3 4 5	× 1	....
12 Confidence when negotiating	1 2 3 4 5	× 1	....
		Total:	....

Use the following questions to ascertain what your rating for each skill should be. Every *no* counts against your rating.

1. Prepare and plan

- Do you always prepare?
- Do you always research the client?
- Do you plan your pricing and extras in advance?
- Do you check who has negotiated with the people before?
- Do you prepare an agenda to structure the negotiation?

2. Give a great first impression

- Do you create a positive impression?
- Do you consider the seating at a face-to-face meeting?
- Are you dressed appropriately, with the appropriate accessories?
- Is your handshake cool and confident?
- Are you smiling or do you look apprehensive?

3. Asking the right questions

- Do you prepare your questions in advance?
- Do you use open questions for information?
- Do you ask closed questions for clarification?
- Do you try to find out what the other side wants?
- Do you re-ask when you are not sure the answers make sense?

4. Listen well

- Do you listen actively and carefully?
- Do you stay in the now – in the present – not thinking of other issues?
- Do you stay quiet and encourage the other side to keep talking?
- Do you nod and ask them to expand?
- Do you use listening, attentive body language?

5. Use your head

- Do you think through the problem on paper?
- Do you brainstorm the issues with others?
- Do you mind map the issues to clarify your thinking?
- Do you know how to keep yourself in a calm state?
- Do you keep a notepad with you at all times to record ideas?

➜

6. Read body language

- Are you always alert to body language?
- Do you notice other people's body language?
- Do you understand the meaning of many body languages?
- Do you mirror and match to gain rapport and a connection?
- Do you manage your own body language at the negotiation table?

7. Watch out for lying

- Are you always alert in case you are being deceived?
- Do you check if you have a feeling that something is not right?
- Do you interpret deception gestures well?
- Are you suspicious if someone is *over* convincing?
- Do you know the verbal clues for lying?

8. Use negotiating tactics

- Do you appreciate the psychology of tactics?
- Do you recognise when tactics are being used on you?
- Do you understand the most common tactics?
- Do you recognise dirty tactics?
- Do you know how to defuse tactics?

9. Influence the other side

- Do you try to build rapport and trust?
- Do you put yourself in the other person's shoes, empathising?
- Do you choose your words and your language carefully?
- Do you have a good idea of the common influencing strategies?
- Do you get commitment before you make a concession?

10. Know how to bargain

- Do you trade concessions?
- Do you never accept the first offer?
- Do you know your variables (extras) to trade?
- Do you use language: 'If you do this – then we will do that?'
- Do you practise haggling in shops and markets to improve your skills?

11. Know how to handle conflict

- Do you ask for more than they expect?
- Do you create a little conflict to get what you want?
- Do you know your natural conflict style?
- Do you know how to recognise other styles?
- Do you know that you should change your style to match the other person?

12. Confidence when negotiating

- Do you prepare in order to feel confident when negotiating?
- Do you take an observer, a team member, with you to help your confidence?
- Do you know how to put yourself in a confident state?
- Have you learnt from others about research and confidence?
- Are you aware not to look too over confident?

You might be wondering why there is a different multiplier for some skills. This is because each skill carries a different weight of importance. I have calculated these scores over 25 years of negotiating, refining and honing these questions and the weightings.

For example, preparation carries a weighting of 4 compared with questioning skills, which, whilst important, does not have the crucial importance of the preparation stage in the overall outcome of the negotiation.

What is your score?

- *80 and over* – you are an excellent negotiator. Are there any skills that could be improved? You should focus on those.

- *70–79* – you are a good negotiator. You might have a few areas to work on to achieve the next level.

- *60–69* – you are OK.

- *50–59* – there is room for improvement. There are probably several skills you could improve.

- *40–49* – you want help. You are a below average negotiator and really could develop your skills to improve. What is it that you need to focus on?

- *39 or less* – read this book from cover to cover!

Remember, this is your judgement on where you are now. What is more important is where do you want to be? Where should you be? Bearing in mind you are reading this book to become a better negotiator.

Which skills could you improve?

Looking at your individual scores here will show if any of your skills need special attention. Improving individual skills will help to improve your all-round skills and negotiation. These results will show what techniques you need to work on individually, which directly will affect the negotiation result.

Look at where your weaknesses are – and think about how you are going to strengthen them – as you read through this book.

Recap

- Keep your negotiating score in mind when reading the rest of the book.

- Consider which skills you need to improve.

- Re-score yourself at any time (see Chapter 17).

5.
Who has the power?

In this chapter you will learn:

- That you have to think where the real power is!
- Power can be just a perception.
- How to accept and handle power plays.

Introduction

Power is a key variable when negotiating.

Power is important. However, people without power need to think about how they might create some power or change the perception of the power.

The perception of power

There appears to be a psychological defence mechanism built into a large majority of people, to focus on their weaknesses rather than their strengths. A cannot do mindset rather than a can do.

This can have real consequences in negotiating. If you are one of those many people who focus on their weaknesses, you might assume, naturally, that you are in a weaker position than others when negotiating. Therefore, often you might not ask, for fear of being rejected.

This is not logical. If the majority are doing this, then no wonder it is easy for the more sophisticated negotiator to get a good deal.

The real question is – how do you persuade people where the real power is when you are negotiating?

I mention this every time I speak to audiences and I can see the body language of most people, most of the time, agreeing with me. When

I am with a coaching client, most of my job is to increase the real and the perceived power they have when negotiating.

How can we change our position to be more powerful, reduce their perception of their power and therefore increase our position, our positioning and our confidence?

One of the ways is always to have or create three options, three choices of what or how you will decide, either as a seller or as a buyer.

> *'Let us never negotiate out of fear, but let us never fear to negotiate.'*
> JOHN F, KENNEDY, US PRESIDENT IN THE COLD WAR, 1962

Reality TV programmes

Just look at the business television programmes that are appearing all over the world. They are called *Dragons' Den* or something similar.

The novice entrepreneur goes in and presents their idea and they get taken for the softest deal, which the rich business people can negotiate.

Yes, it is venture capital; yes, they are business angels; and yes, this type of money comes at a price, but let us look at the scenario.

The only business ideas that get accepted are really good. The synergies are good and the rich business people know they are onto a winner. Yet they want a larger slice of the action than they might get, because they have the power, the prestige and the money.

Occasionally, you see someone stand up to them and get a larger slice of the pie.

> *'The person with the most options gets the best results.'*
> THE LAW OF REQUISITE VARIETY

When you are in a situation where you cannot get a feel for where the power is or where you feel weak, the best thing to do is think through the situation. Talk to people. Take advice but do not pay heavily for it. Be careful from whom you seek advice. Make sure they are real experts.

Remember, always get advice from someone experienced who has been there and done it.

WARNING!
Power can be a perception in your mind. Take a reality check.

Power plays

This is where someone tries to dominate the negotiation by psychological moves to make you feel in a weaker position than you really are.

Here is a story about someone my client used to work with. If you go to her offices she keeps you waiting for 20 minutes while you sit outside the room and she has a meeting about your product with her team. She has an aggressive handshake and does not engage in small talk.

Another client of mine sells baby products to major UK retailers, and often has to travel from York to London to see the buyer. However, on several occasions, he has travelled down and found the buyer is too busy to see him. They do not phone ahead to apologise or rearrange to make time in their schedule. They also make out-of-hours phone calls to ask questions about the products.

Many negotiators always will want the other side to feel they are in a weaker position. That is their game plan. While the two people use different tactics, what they are doing adds up to hard negotiation – they manage to win the negotiation at a big cost to you.

How can you avoid power plays?

1. *Stay focused on the goal* – do not let dirty tricks affect your focus.

2. *Be totally prepared* – get yourself in the right frame of mind for the negotiation and have options ready.

3. *Mirror your client* – act as much like them as you can without being confrontational. In other words, mirror their body language, their voice tonality, but avoid confrontational language, unless you are playing back the words they use. (Be careful.) Remember, people like people similar to themselves.

4. *Respond confidently to their questions* – getting back to them when you cannot answer them.

5. *Do not accept unrealistic time pressure deadlines.*

6. *Be reasonable* – do not react in anger; stay calm.

7. *Make sure you want to deal with them and their company* – if you do, make sure you get a realistic deal with a good return on investment.

8. Finally, *think outside the box*; be creative to find solutions to increase your power. The answers to difficult situations need time out and a little space to get our brain juices flowing.

Join these nine dots up, with four straight lines without taking your pen off the paper. The answer is at the end of this book.

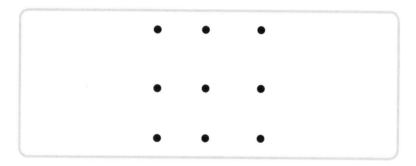

Recap

- There are many ways of changing power. Think outside the box.

- Options create power. Make sure you have three options.

- The Law of Requisite Variety says the person with the most options gets the best results. Information is power.

- Be aware of power plays; they are there to make you feel weaker.

PART 2
THE 11 STEPS OF NEGOTIATION

6.
Prepare and plan

In this chapter you will learn:

- How to find out as much information as possible.
- To look at your starting positions carefully.
- Techniques to consider where they are coming from.
- How to craft your options and positions in advance.
- How to sort out where you are, before you meet the other side.

The importance of preparation

'The more I practise the luckier I get.'
GARY PLAYER

Preparation is the key that creates a successful negotiation. There is no substitute for taking some time beforehand to get all the facts and consider your options. At the same time, you should consider the negotiation from the other side: how might they play their hand?

The bad news here is that there is no shortcut to preparing for a negotiation. For the very best results, you must prepare in full.

The preparation process

Let us look at the preparation stage.

Here are some practical steps:

1. Identify what your goals are. What do you want to achieve from the negotiation?

2. Identify what offers or positions are acceptable to you and your company. What are our positions?

3. Identify any issues you need to be aware of.

4. Prepare an agenda.

If you have negotiated with the other side before, use that knowledge to think about how they might negotiate this time. Remember, people usually behave in the same way.

Their negotiation technique

Do they start high and come down?

Do they play hardball?

Do they tell the truth?

Do they blatantly lie or do they just spin things a little?

Do they expect our first offer to be the real one?

Do they play games?

How do they use tactics?

Do they come down in small amounts?

Have they got a time issue?

Have we got a time issue?

What negotiable variables do they have?

What negotiable variables do we have?

Should we use ploys?

Can we soften them up?

Do we have enough what ifs?

Their financial position

Have they got any financial issues?

Do we think they are under pressure from their bank?

What do the credit rating agencies say?

What does their balance sheet say?

Their online savvy

What does their website look like? Modern and up-to-date?

When did they last blog?

What does their Twitter feed look like?

Look at key individuals' LinkedIn pages

What other social media do they use?

Look at it all – SlideShare, Facebook, etc.

What might you glean from this that might give you a clue into the way they behave in business or negotiate?

Their products

What do their competitor products look like?

How do they compare with your client?

Is there a new model coming out?

Is their equipment/kit looking a little obsolete?

What is the service record?

Their values

Do they practise win win win?

Does their track record stand up to scrutiny?

Are they ethical?

Are they environmentally sound?

What does their environmental policy say?

What accreditations do they have?

ISOs?

Are their key people members of any professional bodies?

Our negotiation strategies

Should we role play this in real time?

Might we record it and play it back? This would show us how we come across.

Who do we know that we can speak to, to find out more about where they are coming from?

Have we really researched this properly?

Are there any cultural issues we have not thought about?

Do we need a team?

What will the team role be?

Where is the power?

> **T!P TOP TIP!**
> Remember the iceberg principle – 90 per cent of the issues are not always apparent; they are below the surface.

The importance of positions

One of the most important but, I find, the least thought about issues in the preparation stage is:

Working out your own positions before going into the negotiations.

At the same time, it is very useful to consider the other side's position and where they might be coming from.

In a negotiation often there are a number of possible outcomes that will be acceptable to both sides. This is the zone of potential agreement (ZOPA) where your mutual positions overlap.

Figure 6.1 The zone of potential agreement (ZOPA)

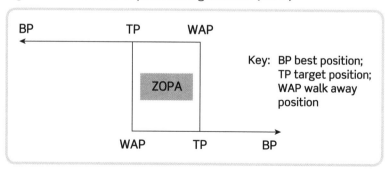

The top line is you and the bottom line is your where you think, estimate, that the other side might be.

However, as you can see, in the ZOPA there are areas that are more beneficial to you and less beneficial to the other side, as well as areas that are less beneficial to you and more beneficial to the other side. This is why it is important to have options set before you start the negotiation.

Have three options (plus the alternative option!)

There are always three options.

If you do not have three options, create them. These are likely to be:

1. *Best position* (BP) – the one you want, in an ideal world.

2. *Target position* (TP) – a softer, more realistic, option.

3. *Walk away position* (WAP) – where you leave the table.

Plus, there is your alternative position. The alternative position is the circumstances that you will be faced with if, and when, you walk away. It has, in the past, been called a BATNA, which stands for best alternative to a negotiated agreement. By understanding and calculating the consequences in cost and time of walking away (your alternative position), it will make you more confident and self-assured.

> **T!P TOP TIP!**
> Sometimes you just have to walk away!

Brainstorm the options that you have. Think outside the box.

Consider the options the other party in the negotiation has, where they are coming from, what they want and how they might play their cards. Check and recheck.

Remember, there are always options. It is a great idea when you are negotiating to list three options that you have on a piece of paper. Consider how you can develop these options to increase your power.

So, the first thing to consider is your best position.

1. What is your best position (BP)?

This is the best position you might obtain. Your dream position. The one that covers all your costs, your research and development, all your overheads and gives you a really good profit margin.

It is important to look at this carefully because you might price yourself out, if the client is comparing you to other suppliers who have similar products. However, when you lose business to the competition, this tells you about your pricing.

For example – products that are priced at typically high prices are usually from companies like Apple, Mercedes and Aston Martin. These companies can command a dream price because their products are so bespoke, so different or are perceived to be so different by branding and marketing.

With my own speaking and consulting business, I test the price points periodically to see what I might obtain with my skills, compared to other consultants and professional speakers in the marketplace.

2. What is your target position (TP)?

This is the position that we would be pleased to receive. One that makes us a nice profit but is market-based and covers all our costs.

Many people start their negotiations here, which can be a mistake if you are selling a bespoke service or a high-value, high-perceived value product.

WARNING!
Fail to prepare – prepare to fail.

3. What is your walk away position (WAP)?

This is the position where we will walk away from the negotiating table and seek another option. Often, it can be difficult to know where the position is because we may not have apportioned our costs correctly: fixed costs, variable costs, marginal costs, etc.

We might want to buy ourselves a little time but make it clear we are walking away.

So, it is good to have a hard and soft walk away.

A *hard walk away position* would be where we say, 'I am sorry. That is our final offer. We cannot go any lower than that or higher than that in any circumstances. That is it.' Your language does not imply that the door might be still open, if circumstances change.

A *soft walk away* would be where we say, 'I am sorry. We cannot go any lower than that today.' The key word is *today*, which buys you a little time, if you are driving back from the meeting and thinking to yourself, I wonder if we got the costs right. It gives you chance to check the spreadsheets, gives you time to reflect on what has happened and gives you time to get others to look at the numbers again.

If you have made a mistake, or have realised there are extra costs that you have not thought of by walking away (there might be extra redundancy costs, if you have to lose people), then you could ring up the next morning and make an extra reduction. I would always advise on it being conditional, getting something in return. For example – 'I have been reflecting and checking the numbers overnight. If you can give us an extra seven days' credit, then we could reduce our price to X.' The condition is the extra seven days' credit.

> **TIP TOP TIP!**
> Sometimes you have to bite the bullet and walk away.

Example of your three different positions

Let us say you are a wedding/event organising company and you are organising a really special wedding in a grand old castle.

1. *Your best position (BP)*, which includes a big profit margin and extras where there are big mark ups, like expensive cutlery, plates and canapés before the meals, etc., might be £200,000. You might make it £196,000 for cosmetic reasons. The £4,000 less looks much cheaper than the £4,000 you are losing.

2. *Your target position (TP)* might be £185,000, less profit and slightly downgraded extras.

3. *Your walkaway position (WP)* might be £174,000, where your profit is small. You might have left smaller items out of the smaller package.

However, with any contract like this where there are a number of variables, it is better to leave the door open by using soft language – 'That is the best we can do in the circumstances today/for now/on the specifications you have asked for/on the specifications we have in the quote.'

What is our alternative position (AP)?

If your best position, target position and walkaway position do not work, then your last case should be your *alternative position*. What is the cost or the lost opportunity cost if you walk away? What will we do instead? What will do with our unused resources? What will it cost us not to fulfil this contract?

In the wedding example, we have fixed costs of our office, our permanent staff, bank interest on the cutlery and crockery that we might have bought, whether we fulfil the wedding contract or not. The big question is will we get another wedding on that day, so our freed up time will be invested in marketing for another wedding?

Analysing the costs of not doing the contract, the alternative position, can be a good way of checking your walk away position. It may be that it is worth more to you in the long run to lose money now, but gain trust with the other side.

Recalculate your figures if you are going to lose the business.

I was working with a client who was renegotiating a contract to process cheques at a Northampton factory. There were two other companies bidding to win the contract.

My client was charging 4p to process the cheques, which was about the market rate. We knew that one company was lowballing the price, so we reduced our price to 3.675p per cheque as our best price (BP). Our target price (TP) was 3.5p and our rock bottom walk away price (WAP) 3.25p.

Our alternative position (AP), which we were not contemplating, was to close the factory and make the processers redundant.

We got a phone call from the client, who told us that one processer had quoted 1.5p per cheque. We were shocked, as we knew they would lose a great deal of money doing it at that price. We told the finance director we knew that to be the case because they had the same machinery, same operating costs and same staff costs.

We were told we had three days to reconsider our pricing, so we looked at the numbers again. However, it would not work, and we had to make the decision to walk away. This, ultimately, meant a loss of jobs at the factory and £95,000 in redundancies and idle machinery, but, if we had matched the price, we would have lost over £400,000 a year.

The moral of the story is:

Weigh up the short- and long-term effects of matching a low price or offer.

Many textbooks call the alternative position your BATNA. This comes from the original work of the Harvard Negotiating Project (whose mission is to improve the theory and practice of conflict resolution and negotiation by working on real world conflict intervention, theory building, education and training, and writing and disseminating new ideas).

If you do not get agreement, what is the best thing you will do, without the specific agreement?

T!P TOP TIP!

A best alternative to a negotiated agreement (BATNA) is the same as an alternative position (AP).

We need to understand these positions, both our position and the position of the other side.

Internal negotiations on a client issue can take, and sometimes need to take, as much time as the external negotiations. What I mean is, if you have to reduce your pricing to a figure below the norm because of the circumstances of the contract, and you believe you will still make a useful profit.

Then, persuading your people might take some time. You also want a BP/TP/WAP to be able to negotiate when you are at the table.

If you believe the business is at serious risk from a competitor, it is best to soften up the senior people so they know of the circumstances.

No one likes surprises. You do not want to be the messenger who gets shot, because you did not warn them earlier and give them a chance to adjust the WAP.

> **T!P TOP TIP!**
> Sort out your internal negotiations – your positions – before you go to see the other side.

How can we make a business judgement on their position?

Do as much research into the marketplace as possible. Find out what the competitors are charging. Find out how they sell their goods. What processes do they use? Make enquiries. Ask good questions. If you are interviewing people, find out whatever you can. Ask people in your network who you know well enough to be able to ask.

Go to local networking events where you will meet people who have more information than you.

Where do we think their BP/TP/WAP/AP positions are?

> **T!P TOP TIP!**
> Get as much information as you can. Information is power. The more information you have, the more options you have.

What are your unique selling points (USPs)?

Unique selling points have become jargon for what is special about you.

Unique is a little over used and often the points in USPs are not unique to just you. However, when you are negotiating, it is important that you emphasise the really powerful parts in your argument, which might include using you, what you get from this deal and knowing the unique selling points of you or the business you are representing.

USPs are similar to the value proposition of you and the business you are representing, that is, the good things the client gets from using you.

> **T!P TOP TIP!**
> In a hugely competitive market, the key USP is *you* and your people. The way you serve, look after and service the clients.

How to role-play an important negotiation

Going to a room where you can role-play the negotiation with your colleagues can be very effective.

One person or one team plays you and the other person/team plays the client.

A powerful tool is to set up a camera in the corner.

Often, when I do this with clients, issues arise that we had not thought about. It gives you a chance to look at what you and your team look like and sound like and see how you come across to the other side. See how the body language comes across, how you handle pressure and how you might handle it differently after review.

It is better to do this in a safe environment and improve rather than do it in a live environment when there is a contract at stake.

What are your negotiable variables?

Negotiable variables are small inexpensive items that cost one side very little but are more valuable to the other side.

Negotiable variables are sometimes called:

- inexpensive valuable concessions
- bargaining opportunities that are tradable (BOTTs)
- negotiables.

In negotiations and in businesses everyone has variables. Both sides often can think that their variables are not valuable and often can think that the other side's variables are valuable.

When you are bargaining, you need to know all your variables.

Having your negotiable variables in mind when you negotiate any situation is a prerequisite of your preparation.

Examples of variables

1. *Different types of pricing*:
   payment terms – 30 days, 60 days, 90 days
   > payment date of invoices
   > delaying/deferring/bringing forward/part payments
   > length of contract.

2. *Advice*:
   management time
   > site visits
   > advice on purchasing, staff issues, etc.

3. *Service*:
   extras as part of the service
   > access outside usual hours – personal mobile phone numbers (rather than business mobiles) for emergencies or big opportunities
   > guaranteed speed of response
   > named account executives
   > professional speakers
   > training advisers
   > management consultants.

4. *Information*:
   sharing books on information
   > press cuttings on items of mutual interest.

5. *Personal agendas*:
   hospitality
   > corporate gifts
   > introductions
   > networking
   > sales coaching
   > 1:1 coaching and mentoring
   > ideas
   > personal friendships.

There are lots more.

In your preparation stage, make sure you brainstorm all your options.

Take five minutes to write down what your variables are.

Your negotiable variables

Relative value is a term used to describe perceived value. We all put different values on different things. Value is a perception. It is the seller's job to increase the perceived value and the buyer's job to reduce the perceived value.

Relative/perceived values

Here is an example of how a tray might have a different perceived value, depending on where it is sold:

- In a department store, it might be priced at £20.
- In a big, expensive, branded London store, such as Harrods, it might be priced at £100.
- In a car boot sale, it might be priced at £1 or less.

Same tray, same condition; different marketing and a different perceived value in the different locations.

How might you do this for your own products and services?

You might do it via:

- the packaging
- the way you present it
- your branding strategy
- your first impressions.

We always need to think that value is a perception and look at the way companies like Apple brand and package their products for maximum value.

> **T!P TOP TIP!**
>
> Remember the 6Ps:
>
> proper
>
> preparation
>
> prevents
>
> pretty
>
> poor
>
> performance

The final part of the preparation stage before we go to the negotiation is the agenda for the meeting. Here is some practical advice on agendas.

> **T!P TOP TIP!**
>
> Make sure you have a clear, focused agenda.

Meeting agendas

Agendas are very powerful in controlling situations. They have unique advantages: by suggesting an agenda in advance, they can make you look very professional; at the same time, they can enable you to do three tactically important things:

1. Put the items on the agenda for your tactical advantage.

2. Send the agenda to the other side in advance.

3. Find out who will be at the meeting from the other side.

1. Put the items on the agenda for your tactical advantage

For example, I always recommend you put background as the number one item. Why? This is because it does not actually mean anything specific. It is so the other side might start talking and tell you things that you did not know, almost voluntarily; things that will be useful in your decision-making process when you make offers and counter offers.

If they say nothing, then you can start the meeting with some small talk around the issues and move on to item number two.

The next few points tactically should be items that both sides are likely to agree on. Why? Because agreement creates trust and momentum. Both are very important in negotiating, as we know.

The contentious issues, the issues that need hard negotiating, ought to be left until about three quarters of the way through the agenda. Why? Because, if you already have six or seven points agreed, you have built up momentum. You can say we have made a lot of progress, we have only two items where we are apart. Note the positive language, to continue the momentum of agreement.

Now I might recommend you say, 'Let's park those items on one side and go on to the other items. We will come back to them at the end.' You can see where I am going, can't you? At the end, you might have eight items agreed and only two items that you disagree on. It's the 80/20 rule again (see Chapter 10).

Even if these items are mammoth, and you are a million miles apart, both sides know you have spent time on all the other items and they are agreed.

This is a much better way of going about it than getting stuck on item number one and not moving.

How do you deal with it if you do get stuck on number one and, by mistake, you were not able to control the agenda? Say, 'Could we park it on one side?' When I say that, I tend to use my hands, as if I am picking the item up and physically moving it to another part of the desk.

Another technique you might use is to have a flip chart available. I always recommend you have a flip chart in any negotiating room, and write the outstanding issues (note the positive language, rather than the issues we disagree on) on the flip chart so everyone can see. This will satisfy them they are there to come back to.

2. Send the agenda to the other side in advance

Why? This has two benefits:

1. It shows them that you are professional.
2. It gives them the chance, and you ask them to do this, to send you any items that they would like added.

You do not ask them if they want the order of the agenda changed. But, if they ask for the order to be changed, you agree, immediately. This shows that you are compliant to their requests, and also gives you some thinking time as to why they wanted the order changed.

It might tell you that these are important issues to them. It might tell you that they are making a point that you are not controlling the meeting or the agenda (it can be a good idea, sometimes, when you know you are up against strong, macho, alpha types or even narcissistic-styled people).

When the other side tells you they want items added to the agenda, this gives you two benefits:

1. They might be items that you had not been aware of. We need to know as much information in advance so we can prepare for the unexpected. Knowing that there is an item we had not thought of gives us the chance to research it and find out the facts.
2. If they raise a complaint in the meeting that you were not aware of, as some competitive negotiators might do deliberately, then, justifiably, you can say that it was not on the agenda, you were not aware of it, so you might have to adjourn the meeting or park that point so that you can identify it, research it and get back to them. You are taking the point off line, outside of that meeting.

3. Find out who will be at the meeting from the other side

One final point on the agenda – make sure you know who is going to be at the meeting from the other side!

Personal agendas

As opposed to the meeting agenda, this final section refers to personal, hidden agendas and political agendas. These are issues that, unless we have built up a good relationship with the individuals, we are unlikely to know about.

Examples of personal agendas might include:

- 'I have to show the boss I am a good negotiator and I have to take points back to the office that I have won.'
- 'I am leaving the company soon, so I need all the help from people like you when I go into my own job.'
- 'I need to be seen by my colleagues at the meeting as a tough no compromising person, even though I am not.'
- 'I hate negotiating. So, if you could let me win something I will concede everything else and back off.'
- 'I take everything personally, that is the way I am. So, if you agree to what I need to take back, I will not ask for any more.'
- 'I like you and I would like to ask your advice on some personal things, like getting a new job.'

Finally, you may find that, through relationship building in the negotiation, the other side starts to trust you more and more. They may start sharing more information about their personal lives.

Do not be surprised about this. They trust you, and want to get to know you better. This means they are less likely to use a hardball position with you, but it also means that you should be careful that you do not use information against them.

Recap

- Remember the 6Ps – proper preparation prevents pretty poor performance.
- Prepare your three offer positions in advance.
- Consider their three likely offer positions.

- You have to have a walk away position.
- Check what you are both really trying to achieve.
- How can you prepare to make it a win win win?

> **T!P TOP TIP!**
> Sometimes you should walk away if the results are not going to be worth the reward, the hassle or the time.

7.
Give a great first impression

In this chapter you will learn:

- Why first impressions are very important when negotiating.
- How you look and act matters.
- How to prepare for a great first impression.

Introduction

We form impressions about new people and companies in a very short time and it is quite difficult to change those opinions once formed. Therefore, managing impressions or impression management is very important in life business and, particularly, negotiations.

When you are negotiating, you are attempting to influence the other side/person to come round to your way of thinking and get them to move further away from their position and nearer to yours. If you have made a bad first impression, then you will have to do a lot more work to move them to your side, but, if you have made a great first impression, then the good news is that you are half way there.

We need to make sure we have done everything we can, to ensure a good impression is created to help the process towards what we want.

How long do you have to make a first impression?

Back in 1974, the belief was that you had four minutes to make a first impression. However, some people now say you only have four seconds, and others say it is a nanosecond. There are many views and no one is really sure of the answer, but my experience tells me it is a very short time – probably around three seconds. In those three seconds the other people are studying you: working out what sort of person you are, what sort of team you have with you and how easy it might be for them to get their own way, get agreement or just get on with you.

What is also crucial is that, once a first impression is made, it is embedded and very difficult to shift. This means that, during the first 3–30 seconds, you must do all you can to enhance the first impression you make. That will, almost certainly, affect the way they behave in the negotiation, depending on whether they feel you might be hostile, aggressive, soft, compliant, etc.

Some people have low emotional intelligence (EI) on these facts, but professional negotiators have to learn to have their radar/antennae switched on to pick up the vibes and manage the situations to their own benefit.

So, how do you ensure you make a first impression that will help your outcome?

First of all, you have to remember always that first impressions are vital. This is your mindset. After all, never forget, you do not get a second chance to make a first impression.

How you look and act matters

Dress for success

You might think this is common sense, but plan what you are wearing to suit your negotiation. Bear in mind who you are going to meet, what they are like, what the company is like and the place in which you are meeting.

I like to wear a red tie as part of my negotiating uniform, but, if I think that colour might be seen as too aggressive, then I tone the colour down a bit. I like the energy that red gives and its business connection.

TIP TOP TIP!
Top negotiators dress for success. Dress for the situation and the people at the meeting.

Why am I recommending you do this? Because of the people like me (PLM) syndrome. People like people who are like them. They are influenced more easily by people who they perceive to be more like them. In fact, it is very difficult to influence someone who does not like you.

So, when we are negotiating, it helps enormously to have the person like you. Therefore, when we set up the first impression, the more we can do to get the person to like us, the more effective we will be in our negotiating outcome.

T!P TOP TIP!

When people like us, they are more likely to give us more information, allow us to ask more difficult questions and give us more frank answers.

If all is equal in a competitive situation, sale, pitch, negotiation, the decision probably is going to be made in favour of the person or the people they like and trust the most.

Arriving at the negotiating meeting place

Here there are some key things to consider both from your perspective and from the other side's perspective.

Get there in plenty of time. Do not be late. This means you will be in the right state for the meeting: cool, calm and prepared. Get out of your car, have a stretch, take three large breaths and remind yourself how good you are and what you have done in the past.

Go into the reception 10 minutes early, talk to the receptionist or whoever meets you, build rapport, and engage in a little small talk, where appropriate.

It is always useful when you sign the visitors' book to see if anyone else has been in before you, in case you can find out about the competition, or any advisers they have: solicitors, lawyers, accountants, who might have got there early for a pre-negotiating meeting. This gives you more information – and, remember, information is power. It can tell you who you are in competition with.

T!P TOP TIP!

Always consider standing in the reception area.

I am often asked why you should consider standing in the reception area. There are three reasons:

1. You want to be in the right physical and mental state when you meet the person. Standing up straight, ready to go will keep you in this frame of mind.
2. It stops you focusing on other things, like emails and anything on your smartphone.
3. When the person comes to meet you, you are there, at eye level, connecting with them.

These are great rules for any business. The smarter you are on impressions, the more you will be able to negotiate. Because your prices will start higher and, if necessary, you will have further to come down – more to play with!

> **T!P TOP TIP!**
> These tips are very useful to you. Focusing on the impression you make, and that of your business, will give you the opportunity to keep prices high and leave room to negotiate lower, if necessary.

WARNING!
You never get a second chance to create a first impression.

Seating – where might you sit?

One of the important issues to make the negotiation easier is where you sit. When you walk into the negotiating room, you can see immediately how the seating has been set up.

It is best not to sit across the desks, looking at each other. This is confrontational and, the further away from the other side you are, the more confrontational it is. Subliminally, it looks like a hardball negotiation, almost set up for a win/lose.

It is best to try and seat either round a round table (but most offices have rectangular tables) or across the end of desks. This makes it easier to build rapport with the other side. It looks and feels more like you working together in a win win scenario.

So, if you are first in the room, this is what I would recommend. You place your papers at the end of the table, but do not sit down. Wait for the people to arrive and then, if they sit close to you in a good position, great. If they do not, you can pick up your papers and move around. If it is your office, you can invite them to sit in a particular position.

As long as your strategy is win win win, you might be able to make a little joke like, 'We are all working together for a win win win outcome, aren't we? Shall we sit together?' It is difficult for the other side not to do that, unless they are being really aggressive and their goal is not win win win.

REASONS FOR NOT SITTING DOWN
Once seated, it is difficult to move. If you are sitting down, you are lower than the people entering the room. By standing up, you keep your body in a more confident position, which means that you will feel more confident. Standing with good confident posture sends hormones and endorphins to the brain, which increases confidence.

This is another reason not to sit down in a reception area. You can also practise confident body language. See the piece of research from Harvard psychologist Amy Cuddy online at www.youtube. watch?v=Ks-_Mh1QhMc.

Rapport

We talk more about rapport in Chapter 11. However, the view is that you might make the first few minutes of the meeting for small talk, building rapport before you get down to the business of the negotiation. This helps the ambiance and helps everyone to feel at ease.

I heard the researchers at Harvard saying that the first 10 minutes of any negotiation are crucial to the way it would turn out. I was not surprised.

They had worked on resolving crucial issues around the world since the Harvard Negotiating Project was set up in the late 1980s. Some of these had been in conflict zones such as Israel and Palestine.

They had seen situations where the negotiators had spent no time with small talk to connect with the other side, being respectful of their cultures and their ways.

What they learnt here was that:

- Time is important to some cultures.
- Getting the small things right is vital.
- The food and drinks for both sides are important.
- The cultural customs can make or break situations.
- Putting yourself in the other side's shoes is crucial.

> **T!P TOP TIP!**
> Impressions are like quick-drying cement: once formed they are very difficult to change.

So what should you be looking for in those split seconds?

I visited a firm of headhunters in London and one of its directors told me that she forms an impression of a candidate in a split second.

To make sure they are not too prepared, she meets the candidates at the lift, so they are taken by surprise and typically she would look at:

- eyes – for energy and attitude
- smile – for genuineness and positivity
- handshake – for touch and feel
- shoes – for cleanliness.

All in a nanosecond. This gives her an insight into the person. After all, she will be negotiating with them and for them, if she takes them on as a client. She needs to know now if the person is a good prospect. Now.

T!P TOP TIP!

Research into criminal trials shows that jurors make their mind up about the accused in the first 10 minutes and it is very difficult to change their minds.

THE ECONOMIST

What can you tell from handshakes?

I have noticed and observed people's handshakes for a number of years. This is after I became curious why people who behaved aggressively or had a bullying style of leadership seemed to try and put their hand on top of mine. Alternatively, initially they might shake hands in a normal position and then turn my hand.

I concluded, from many negotiations, that they were dominant people who felt they needed to win.

So, when it happened, I noticed it, noted it and then, when it came to pricing or points to concede, I made sure I had enough room to manoeuvre that I allowed them to win. Sometimes it meant I had to increase my position initially so that they could think they had won more.

Similarly, someone who crushes your hand is also making a point. It tells you that probably they have lower emotional intelligence than normal. A good handshake should be upright, with your thumb pointing up, firm and at about the same strength as the person you are shaking hands with.

Generally, women have a 30 per cent less strong handshake – and, therefore, if you are a man, you should adjust to the strength you feel at that point.

Remember that many of the things I am mentioning here are below the conscious awareness of most people most of the time. However, they tell you little things about the type and style of the person you are negotiating with.

My wife often takes her ring off her right hand when she is shaking hands with men, when we meet them at social occasions. Why? Several times she has almost had her finger broken by the strength of a male handshake.

WHAT YOU MIGHT DO?
Ask someone to rate your handshake on a scale of 1–10. Ask them what they notice. A good influencer will go in with a slightly open handshake and notice how and what the other person does.

Reminders

Before every negotiation you should cover the following checklist:

Appearance and attitude

What do I need to do to be professional?

Am I groomed properly?

Have I dressed for success?

Make sure I am in the appropriate mental state for the meeting.

The meeting

Do I have the correct address?

What time should I arrive?

Do I know who is attending?

Is the agenda prepared?

What is on the agenda?

It could be an advantage to send it in advance, and ask for anything that they would like to add.

Do I have everything I need?

Do I have copies of any relevant paperwork?

Do I have the right accessories, pen, notebook, briefcase, etc.?

Recap

- Dress appropriately to suit the meeting.
- Put yourself in a positive frame of mind (state) for a win win win outcome.
- Set your goals.
- Be ready to impress from the moment you are near the meeting place.
- Stay on your feet when waiting, so you are alert.
- Be ready to smile and give a firm handshake.
- Use appropriate small talk to build rapport.
- Sit side by side, not facing each other, to be more cooperative.

8.
Ask the right questions

In this chapter you will learn:

- Why asking good questions is so important when negotiating.
- How to phrase really good questions.
- Types of questions you might ask.
- Why it is good to be curious.
- How to keep digging.
- What to do after you have asked a question.

Why asking good questions is so important when negotiating

Questions are vital to the negotiation process. Everybody has different views about the issues they are negotiating, especially given our different and varied opinions and goals.

So, therefore, in a negotiating situation, asking good or great questions will enable you to discover as much about the other side's position, views and thinking as possible from their answers.

The ability to ask high-quality questions and then accurately listen with all your senses to the response is an essential skill.

High-quality questions take careful preparation. Usually it is difficult to ask well-constructed tough questions in a gentle non-offensive way under pressure and without preparation. High-quality questions seek out the answer you need to hear in order to determine the truth and the facts on which to base your next steps and eventual decision making.

Observing the answers to these well-prepared questions means listening carefully, watching the accompanying body language for congruence and noticing what is not said.

The use of high-quality questions in a negotiation is vital to getting the right answers to make informed decisions.

Yet, many negotiators ask poor questions and therefore get poor answers.

> **T!P TOP TIP!**
> The quality of the questions you ask determines the quality of the answers you get.

This chapter will show you how to ask really good questions and to listen to the meaning of the answers you get.

Asking enables you to get to the real issues. In negotiating, people who really want to get their own way will not always tell you the truth. They might lie, they might withhold information and they might leave out important information.

To make good decisions, decisions that will take us towards our goals, we must have all the facts. Decisions that are made on only half the facts are poor decisions. We need to be as close to 100 per cent of the facts as possible before we make decisions. This includes before deciding or changing our best position, target position, walk away position and alternative position.

Often, you can see in the news where poor decisions have been made and clearly the big questions have not been asked.

When Lloyds TSB took over HBOS, the directors made their decision within 12 hours. How could they have had time to ask the right questions and receive answers that could have been verified? Often, in negotiations, one side puts pressure on the other side to dispense with due diligence.

In my experience of 33 years in financial services, this should be strongly resisted to ensure that the right decisions are made.

Questions are still being asked now how this could have happened.

Some people are afraid to ask, afraid to embarrass the other person, afraid to embarrass themselves or just afraid of the answer they might get. However when business people do not ask the right questions, then they might deserve what they get, if they get a poor deal.

Of course the bigger the company, the bigger the consequences are for not asking the right questions. The directors are running the company for the benefit of the shareholders, the people who put their money into the company for a return. This is a very responsible position, a position that carries a great deal of responsibility: to ask the right questions and make judgements on the right answers, or the answers that are as near to right as possible.

As a negotiator you must learn to ask questions in a nice way.

> **T!P TOP TIP!**
> Ask difficult questions in a soft tone of voice; ask easy questions with a strong tone of voice.

Appearing on BBC Radio London recently, I was accused by the presenter of being too nice to be a good negotiator. I explained that the most powerful questions could be asked softly. This appeared wasted on the presenter, who wanted to make a point that he thought to be a good negotiator you had to sound tough. You do not, if you ask high-quality questions and probe.

If you do not ask, you do not get

Many people have been brought up by parents being told to ask, and ask politely. The same applies to asking business questions. Asking questions does not mean asking them in an aggressive way, as we might see in a television courtroom drama. All questions, no matter how difficult, can be asked nicely.

Do not assume – ASK

Human nature often dictates that we think that others are coming from the same position as us. This can be a big mistake, which is why assuming information is also a big mistake. In my experience, average negotiators often assume answers to questions, rather than asking the other side. Even if you are fairly sure of the answer, it can be beneficial to hear the answer from the other side.

Here is a great way to remember not to assume or make assumptions. The first three letters of the word assume are *ass*.

Then write down the word *assume – ass u me –* and remind yourself periodically that assume will make an *ass* out of u and me!

> **T!P TOP TIP!**
> If there is any doubt where the other side is coming from, ask. Do not assume anything.

As we know, information is power in any negotiating situation. You could use ASK as an mnemonic:

A – always

S – seeking

K – knowledge

How to phrase really good questions

So, now you know the importance of asking questions, let us focus on what questions to ask. Phrasing really good questions is a skill that anyone can do but it takes preparation, thought and practice. I keep a notebook with me to write down questions as they come to me when I am reflecting on a negotiating situation.

Ask yourself:

- What am I trying to achieve?
- What is the best order in which to ask these questions?
- Are they good, high-quality questions, which will get me to where I want to go?
- Do they help me discover where the other side is coming from?

Types of questions you might ask

Closed questions

Closed questions are those that give you a yes or no answer. Careful use of them should be employed. The danger is that a closed question can allow the other person to avoid the real question, because they are not under any obligation to elaborate further.

Examples of good closed questions:

- So, is there anything else you need to know before we go ahead with the contract?

- Can you state categorically that you have not agreed to anything cheaper than this?

- Shall we get the contract drawn up?

- Should we write down in draft what we have agreed, photocopy it and sign it before we let the lawyers draft the full documents?

Examples of poor closed questions:

- Is our price too expensive?

- Are you in a hurry?

- Do you need an answer tonight?

- Do you have a better price?

Open questions

If you want a longer, more informative answer, then asking quality open questions will help you understand where the other side is coming from.

Good open questions ask one question and allow the other side to think about it and answer in their own time. Generally, they follow the rule of beginning a question with *what, why, where, when, who* and *how* or *tell me about . . .*

This is known often as 5WH.

Examples of high-quality open questions:

- How much have you got in your budget?
- How can we solve this problem?
- How much can you pay?
- How close can you get to our price?

To obtain more information, following open questions, use these examples:

- Could you tell me more about . . . ?
- Please can you expand on that?
- What do you want to achieve here?
- Why is it an issue for you?
- How can we resolve this?
- What are the deal breakers for you?
- And, if they dry up, just say, *'Anything else?'* with an enquiring tone of voice.

So, now we have covered open and closed questions, when should you use them? Here are some general rules for you:

CLOSED QUESTIONS	OPEN QUESTIONS
To clarify a situation when you are not getting a straight answer.	At the beginning of the negotiation to understand their situation.
To confirm your understanding.	To get them talking generally about things.
At the end of the negotiation to close the contract or the written agreement.	When you are not sure of the facts and you want to hear them elaborate.

Let us now get more specific with the 5WHs: why, what, when, why and how.

WHY QUESTIONS
Why do we ask why questions?

> *Why questions are asked to be very specific. To understand the reasons why it is that someone has taken that course of action.*

Why questions have to be chosen more carefully, as the receiver might see them as confrontational or as a personal attack. Additionally, they can trigger thoughts from the past, when we were challenged as children by parents or teachers. This can put us into a negative, low energy state and make your counterpart less forthcoming and open with you.

So, we should be careful how we ask them and consider reframing them to make them a little softer, so they are less blunt and direct.

HARD VERSION	SOFT VERSION
Why did you agree that price?	What was your thinking in agreeing that price?
Why did you speak to her about her salary like that?	What was the outcome you thought you would achieve by speaking to her like that?
Why did you do that deal?	What was your objective in doing that deal?
Why did you make that decision on the key point in the contract?	What was the purpose of deciding on agreeing to that point?
Why did you pay that price?	How did you rationalise paying that price?

The person being questioned might think, 'Why are you challenging me?' and we might be in a defensive, negative loop if we are not careful. So it is good to ask why questions, but they have to be framed carefully so as not to challenge the other person and put them on the back foot.

A friend of mine, Barry, in his training to be a counsellor for the Samaritans, was told never to ask 'Why?' to the people who called the helpline, as it might be a tipping point for them. For example, to ask, 'Why are you feeling so depressed?' might reinforce their negative problem and build it up in their mind.

Why questions can be reframed into more gentle phrases, such as, 'Tell me about the issues.'

Why it is good to be curious

One way you can get round the why dilemma is to use the word curious. Curious is a very powerful, non-threatening word. It is human nature to be curious; just look at how curious small children are.

I am curious why you paid that price.

I am curious how you made that decision.

I am curious how you came to decide on that machine.

Structure your questions carefully. By structuring your questions you can control the agenda, the meeting and, eventually, the outcome.

Examples of When questions

- When do you think you will be able to go ahead?
- When will you put it to your committee?
- When will you have had time to consider the pros and cons of the offer?
- When will the board be satisfied that the outstanding negotiation points have been sorted?

Examples of Who questions

- Who is the decision maker on this contract?
- Who will I need to convince? Can I help you present the case?

- Who will be presenting the proposal?
- Who will sign off the payments?

Examples of Where questions

- Where will the final agreement be signed?
- Where shall we hold the negotiations?
- Where will we find the answers to their outstanding points?
- Where can we find the information we need, so we can go ahead?

Yes tag questions

A yes tag question follows a statement, which is aimed to get the other person to agree with that statement (which is likely), or show their disagreement.

Yes tag questions are designed to encourage the person to agree with you and build rapport.

When asking a yes tag question, you are, effectively, expecting the other person to think 'yes', so, even though they might not say it, more often than not, they will think yes in their mind and perhaps even nod.

Ask yes tag questions only where you anticipate the majority of people will agree. Yes answers tend to create positive momentum.

Examples of yes tag questions:

- It is a fantastic day, *isn't it?*
- We have made considerable progress, *haven't we?*
- We have only three points to agree on now, *don't we?*
- We are going to celebrate our success with this negotiation, *aren't we?*

No tag questions

A no tag question can be used to ascertain whether anything else needs to be answered, before moving on to the next stage of a discussion or closing a negotiation.

Examples of no tag questions:

- Is there anything else you need to know before we go ahead?
- Is there any more research we need to do before we finalise our agreement?
- Is there further preparation we need to do on the structure of the question before we meet the client tomorrow?

Although it might sound negative, no tag questions are really great for progressing through the various stages in a negotiation. Rather than think of it as one long deal, if you break it into smaller stages and confirm that you are both happy at the end of each, you can both feel you are making good progress.

YES TAG QUESTIONS	NO TAG QUESTIONS
It is great we are working together, isn't it?	Is there any more information about the deal you need to know before we go ahead?
We do all want to achieve a win win win situation here, don't we?	Is there any further work we need to do before tomorrow?
We have made a great deal of progress here, haven't we?	Do we need any more information, before we sign the contract?
If we adjourn till the morning, we are sure we can get an agreement at that point, aren't we?	

How to keep digging

If you are getting unsure answers, or their body language looks uncomfortable, you should ask more probing questions. Be open and honest and say:

- You don't look too sure.
- You don't sound like you have cracked it yet.
- Are you really sure?
- It doesn't feel like we have all the answers yet.
- Are you OK with it?

A few years ago, I was working in risk management for a major international bank. We were concerned about the whereabouts of several million pounds of pension fund assets. One of my colleagues, Peter, was sent to interview a charismatic character who was known for his aggressive financial dealings and his bullying nature.

Peter went to see him face to face and ask him if there were any issues with the company pension fund. He asked him directly whether there was any money missing from the fund – a closed question, requiring only a 'yes' or 'no' answer.

The charismatic character answered, 'That would be illegal, Peter, wouldn't it?' in an assertive, dominating and firm tone of voice. (Note the power of the statement followed with a yes tag question.)

My colleague said he was mesmerised with the answer, agreed it would be illegal and failed to follow up. He went away with an uncomfortable gut feeling, as he had failed to resolve the problem.

He regrets, to this day, not following up further, as it was found out a few days later that millions of pounds were missing from the pension fund.

The moral of the story is:

Average negotiators ASSUME answers that may or may not be right.

T!P TOP TIP!
If you ask high-quality questions, you are more likely to discover the real answers.

WARNING!

- If you do not ask, you do not get.
- If you do not ask, you do not give the other person the opportunity to say yes.
- If you do not ask, then the answer will be no.

What to do after you have asked a question

Once you have asked a question, it is really important that you wait for the answer. More often than not, you will get a response immediately, but, if it is a tricky question, then they might not be as forthcoming. In that case, keep quiet and say nothing more, until you get an answer. Be patient!

One mistake, made often, is that after the quality question is asked the person does not hold the silence. They go on and devalue the first question by asking a supplementary question or making a statement, which qualifies the previous question. This can mean the other side forgets the first question or, more worryingly, is able to ignore the first question.

This qualification often comes from natural embarrassment for the person who is being questioned. Do not make that mistake. You are now heading towards being a master negotiator.

It is important to remain silent after asking questions because, if you do not, you will carry on talking and lose the effect of the question.

Many people will then get embarrassed by the silence and qualify the question with something like, 'because it makes a difference to how we go about the process, and how we go about the process means we can make a better case to our colleagues'.

Learn to hold the silence after the first quality question.

EXERCISE

Try sitting in silence with someone you do not know very well for 30 seconds and see how awkward it feels. This is great practice for holding silences for both of you.

Although sitting in silence can feel extremely awkward, it is really useful in negotiating because it can encourage the other side to talk more. And, if they talk more, often you discover something useful.

Good questions coax lengthy and detailed explanations from the other person. If the person cuts the answer short, encourage them, with reassuring nods, ums and supportive questions, such as, 'Anything else?'

If we listen with both eyes *and* both ears, then we get better information to make our judgements.

Often we can keep the conversation going with nods and words, such as 'Yes', 'I understand', 'Keep going' and supportive 'ums' – which are called prompters, designed to keep things moving. They should be accompanied with positive and supportive body language.

What to do when you have asked a really good question

You know it is a good question when it causes the other side to think deeply before answering it. You will know they are thinking deeply by the delay in answering and their 'unsure thinking' body language.

Keep quiet. Hold the silence for however long it takes. The way you can do this is by imagining a question mark in your mind after you have asked the question. The question mark signals that it is the end of the question and you then say nothing else. You hold the silence.

I was reading a book in a business school library, a number of years ago, in which a silence was held for four and a half hours during the Korean War negotiations between the negotiating parties.

As a visiting lecturer at the Henley Business School, a delegate I was teaching on the Senior Executive Strategy Programme told me that he had been party to a union negotiation, where questions were asked and then neither side spoke for nine and a half hours. I said that I had never heard of a silence that long and he assured me that was how long it took.

The stalemate was broken finally when one side called for an adjournment for a week and stopped playing the silence game. 'The first one to talk loses' – the problem with this macho style of negotiating long silences and hard ball positions is that the psychology is 'I win and you lose'. This is not convivial to a win win win scenario.

Looking back on it, it was a waste of time with no winners.

What to do when you think you are being fobbed off!

Drill down. What I mean by this is repeat what you have heard. For example, so what you are saying is . . . ? Say it with a quizzical frown on your face – 'Can you elaborate more?'

The other tactic you might use is to use the Colombo routine (see 'Dumb is smart – the Colombo tactic' in Chapter 13). This is the negotiating tactic made famous in the TV series. For example, 'I am sorry. I think I am being a bit dumb today, but I do not understand. Can you run that past me again? If they say exactly the same, keep digging, saying things like, 'I just don't get it,' etc.

Recap

- Prepare and structure your questions in advance.

- Closed questions get a yes or no answer – good for clarifying situations.

- Open questions are really powerful and generally start with what or how.

- If you do not get a satisfactory answer, re-ask the question in a different way – gently – and watch, listen and sense the accuracy of the answer.

9.
Listen well

In this chapter you will learn:

- Why listening is so important.
- How to stay focused and listen.
- What to do if you are distracted.
- What to do if they are distracted.
- What key words to listen for.
- How to interpret the way they are saying it.

Why is listening so important?

As a negotiator, you need to be a good listener. In fact, I would say you need to be a really good, first-class listener.

You need to understand clearly where the other party is coming from: what they want, what they do not want, their agendas, their hidden agendas and everything there is to know that can be known.

If you are really determined to become a serious negotiator, then first you must become a serious listener.

You will be a better negotiator if you listen well because you will have more information, facts and views at your disposal to make more informed negotiating decisions.

Listening is one of the most difficult skills to do accurately. It needs all of our senses to be employed, to get an accurate picture. You are talking about the ability to listen to what people are saying, what they really mean and what they are not saying. In any negotiation, active disciplined listening is a critical success factor: the ability to really hear what the person is saying.

Generally, most people are poor listeners, most of the time. 'Why is this?' you might ask. You are too busy to listen properly. You rush around and therefore listening is inconvenient. You think you know what the issue is, what the problem is, what the opportunities are and, therefore, you are already preparing your answers. Perhaps you want to avoid boredom.

However, before you get too involved in the practice of listening, you must remember you are listening to the whole person. You are listening to the words, the way they are said, the confidence or the hesitation, the tonality, the body language and what, perhaps, is not said.

 WARNING! THE DANGERS OF NOT LISTENING

- You will miss key information, which will affect the outcome of your negotiation.
- If someone thinks you are not listening to them, they will treat you with less respect and tell you less information.
- You may make wrong assumptions.

Listen with your two eyes and your two ears and speak only with one mouth.

Listen to the language they use, the words they use, the way they say it, the body language that accompanies the words that re-enforce the message or are incongruent to the message.

If you want a great example of hearing without listening, look at this video showing the US Navy misunderstanding a situation: https://www.youtube.com/watch?v=KvRYd8U7qGY.

The point is that listening means asking questions to clarify and really understand the issues.

Good negotiators are good listeners. Great negotiators are great listeners!

What is the difference between hearing and listening? *Hearing* is the sounds and the words.

Listening is the meaning of what the person is saying.

How to stay focused and listen

You might think that you do not have to learn how to listen, but listening skills are far from easy. Active listening needs concentration and total focus.

The average person speaks at around 150 to 200 words per minute.

However, as some people can think at up to more than 800 words per minute, this leaves a lot of space for head-chatter in our mind.

Figure 9.1

A good idea here is to pretend you have a pause button, like on your audio device or computer and imagine you have pressed it. The pause button controls your inner self-talk and your outer verbal talk.

Get in the zone

Before you start listening you should put yourself in a heightened state of awareness:

1. Sit up straight. Be alert and concentrate on the person who is speaking.
2. Mirror and match their body language.
3. Stay silent.
4. Ignore head chatter.

Listen actively

To listen accurately you have to remain silent with your outer voice (what you are saying) and your inner voice (what you are thinking).

1. Switch your attention to them – concentrate 100 per cent on the person speaking.

2. Listen to what is being said and what is not being said.

3. Listen to how they are saying what they are saying.

4. Watch their body language.

5. Use silence to good effect – sometimes not saying something can make them speak more.

6. Use what you hear to ask questions – 'Is there anything else?'

T!P TOP TIP!
Keep a small note on your pad to remind yourself to listen *acutely*.

Avoid jumping to conclusions

Listening to somebody without passing judgement is a great skill.

This means listening but not interpreting what you hear, according to your own life experiences. Humans have a natural tendency to form judgements about people and issues, due to what has happened to us as individuals in the past and the way we have been brought up by our parents or by people who have influenced us at various ages and stages of our development.

For example, our own moral standards could influence how we hear what is being said.

Remember to stay silent with your mouth and listen accurately with your mind.

T!P TOP TIP!
When I am coaching executives to listen in key negotiations, I remind them that *listen* is an anagram of *silent*. They have to remain totally silent not only by avoiding speaking but by avoiding thinking about what they are going to say next.

What if you are distracted?

The real problem that most people have is that listening is a choice. You choose whether you think the message is important and you need to get it right. When you are negotiating, the message is always important because it gives us vital information.

If you are negotiating, then there is no point not listening. If the message is not important, you should ask yourself 'Why am I here?'

Here are just a few reasons why you might be distracted from listening effectively in a negotiation situation:

- You are preoccupied with our own thoughts.
- The other person says something that triggers other thoughts in our mind.
- You are bored by the other person. Anchors and triggers are programmed into us by the experiences of life. Something someone says or does can remind us of something that happened to us in the past and start a train of thought in our mind.
- You do not block out other sounds and noises.
- You have biases, appearances, facts you know about people to cloud your information.
- You are in a hurry – to finish a project or to get to a meeting.
- You have a closed mind to the subject.
- In a meeting, you tune people out because you think they never have a good idea or you just do not like them.
- You do not like what you are hearing.
- Stress (this is one of the biggest reasons why people do not listen).

One of the major difficulties of listening is head chatter. Head chatter is when you have other thoughts and ideas going on in your mind.

Examples of head chatter might be: 'Why is he wearing that ridiculous tie?' 'What am I going to get for dinner?' 'He reminds me of one of my brother's friends.' 'Does she really think that power dressing suit will impress us?'

Here are the key steps to avoid distractions:

1. Focus on the person who is talking.
2. Put away any equipment, such as a mobile device.
3. If on the telephone, blank your computer screen.
4. If in an open plan area, ignore anybody going by.
5. Sit upright, with positive body language.
6. Do not think about what you are going to say next.
7. Do not think about how you are going to respond in advance.

TIP TOP TIP!
Remember that listening is a choice you make.

RAPID REPEAT METHOD
Rapid repeat is a method of listening that can help you stay focused. It is very simple and it works. Simply repeat silently in your mind what is being said, a fraction of a second after it has been said. This holds your concentration and improves your recall of what was said.

Many governments are thinking about how they might have to change laws relating to juries. Why?

It has been discovered that jurors have lost the ability to listen with all the distractions of the internet, television, social media and all the other new twenty-first-century distractions.

Recently, the Lord Chief Justice in the United Kingdom said, 'You have a generation now in the jury box, totally unused to sitting and listening. That changes the whole tradition of aurality with which you are familiar.'

Researchers are suggesting that jurors might be given monitors to take away and they might be able to press buttons to obtain information that they wanted clarification on.

What if they are distracted?

*How can you tell if someone **is** listening to you?*

By reading the other person's body language, you can tell quickly how well the negotiation is going and decide what you need to do next. It is important to pay attention to their body language and keep them engaged, because you want their full attention if you are going to persuade them well.

Check their body language

Body language is covered in Chapter 11, but it is easy to tell via a person's body language whether they are listening to you or not.

Good signs that mean they are listening:

- *Open arms* – this means they are receptive to what you are saying.
- *Comfortable eye contact* – if they pay attention to where you are looking then you have got their attention.
- *Sitting forward* – if they are leaning forward in your direction, they are intent on you.

How can you tell if someone **is not** listening to you?

If someone is not listening to you, it will also be clear from their body language.

Bad signs that mean they are not listening:

- *Crossed arms* – this implies the person is likely not to be listening to the arguments. Now, of course, this is not always the case. They may be uncomfortable, they may be cold, and they may have some real issues on their mind.
- *Poor eye contact.*
- *Too much eye contact* – sometimes people who are not telling the truth or misleading people hold *too much* eye contact when talking to people. Around two seconds is the norm for good contact, but this varies from person to person.

- *They look distracted* – they are doing other things, such as checking their electronic devices.

- *They are distracted* – you can hear a keyboard in the background.

When they are on the telephone, many people think they can cover up not listening and do other things, check emails and not listen, and get away with it. This is far from the truth. To listen accurately you must give 100 per cent concentration. I survey people in my masterclasses and ask this question: 'Can you tell when someone is not listening to you on the telephone?' Almost 95 per cent of people say they can.

As well as what they are doing *physically*, you should think about how their body language relates to what they are saying. Consider: is what they are saying congruent with what they are doing physically? Do the words match the body language? For example, if they are saying that something is true, do they look like they believe it is true? Signs for them not believing it could be nose rubbing, fidgeting, going red, change of skin colour, perspiration. Or are they saying they are happy with the deal, but are looking extremely frustrated?

Are they behaving differently when you talk? If their body language changes completely between when they speak and when they listen, beware. This could mean a number of things. If it is confident, it might mean they are thinking they have done better than they had thought previously. If it is less confident, it could mean they have some concerns about what they have just promised. Can they deliver it?

What we need to do is spot the changes. When we see changes then we might choose to dig deeper with further questions, drawing out more information to make our decision.

What do I do if someone is not listening?

If your fellow negotiator is not listening to you, it is important to do something to get their attention back to the negotiation. Do something for effect, do something different, 'a pattern interrupt', as the psychologists say – to re-energise and bring the person back into the room.

Feel free to address the issue by saying, 'Why don't we take a five-minute break?' Other physical things you could do are: pour some coffee, order some food, open a window, change the way you are sitting.

What key words should I listen for?

When you are listening carefully in a negotiation you will hear key words. Key words could be:

- 'My *normal* price is . . .'
- 'You do not *usually* give discounts.'
- 'It is going to be *difficult* to do that.'
- 'Our policy is almost always . . .'
- 'Only head office can agree . . .'
- 'The manager is the only one with the authority.'
- 'You need a discount facility.'

In the first two cases the key words are *normal* and *usually* and, in the other cases, the question to ask is – *why*?

So I might retort –

'It is our policy not to pay the normal price, we normally expect to get a discount. It is our policy.'

OR – 'We usually insist on discounts.'

OR – 'Why is it going to be difficult? How can you help get round this?'

There are many other keywords to watch out for, depending on the circumstances.

Here are examples of some of them:

- 'At the moment or at the present time we cannot move our position.'
- 'We have a special price coming up.'
- 'It is difficult to move on our current offer.'
- 'This is today's deal.'

In all these cases dig down a bit deeper to see in what circumstances they might be able to move their position.

How are they saying it?

The way people say things is very important. The voice tonality, the emphasis they put on certain words.

Listen for tremors in their voice, which indicate nervousness or lying. Hesitancy probably means they are unsure, as might a stutter when the person does not normally stutter. A soft confident voice could mean they are sure of themselves, whereas the loud bullying type of voice might mean they are not sure.

If they sound vague, probably they are not sure of themselves or the issue you are negotiating. Some people sound scripted. If they are scripted, you can bet they are not listening to your concerns.

Some people are in roles which need to sound assertive: police officers, lawyers, etc. Make sure they are not role-playing what they expect people to hear and check, by asking more questions, whether they really have the facts.

The key, again, is to notice these issues.

REMEMBER TO ASK YOURSELF TO WAIT

WAIT stands for 'Why am I talking?'

You cannot listen and talk. When you find yourself talking, ask yourself, 'Why am I talking?'

Whenever you are negotiating, and remember that everything ends up as a negotiation at some stage, don't forget: 'People who care listen – and people who listen care.' Therefore, if you listen, the other side will like you more and, if they like you, they are likely to tell you more, let you into their secrets, and that means, generally, you will be able to negotiate better agreements, nearer to our goal of win win win negotiation.

Listening is such an important subject in negotiating. By really listening you are discovering where the other side is coming from, what they want, whether there are any hidden agendas, all before you make your offer or change your position.

Try this exercise.

EXERCISE

Ask a friend to talk for one minute; you are not allowed to interrupt. You must listen 100 per cent. Then, after a minute, repeat back to that person what they said.

Then swap places and repeat the exercise so your friend can have a turn.

Most people find this exercise very difficult and quite tiring. The benefits are that it makes you really concentrate on the actual words, the way they are saying them and the body language. You have to practise active, disciplined listening.

T!P TOP TIP!

Remember that most people want a good listening to, not a good talking to.

Recap

- Listen carefully in any negotiation; you will be surprised what you hear.

- *Listen* is an anagram of *silent*. During the negotiation, listen by remaining silent in your head and with your mouth. Take care with any head chatter.

- Make sure you are listening to what the other person is really saying, the real message. That will double your chances of a successful negotiation result.

10.
Use your head

In this chapter you will learn:

- How to use your brain to your advantage when negotiating.
- How to mind map, brainstorm and mind storm for better negotiating results.
- How to use speed reading to get more information in less time.
- How the expression 'Sleep on it' gets better results.

Introduction

This is a key chapter in getting great results in your negotiations.

It supplements many of the points under preparation and it will help you to be more efficient and productive and, therefore, more successful when negotiating. These are also very useful life skills.

Summary of the content:

- Using whole-brain skills – linking skills that use both hemispheres.
- How to use brain filtering to your advantage.
- Why mind mapping is important.
- The RAS – and focusing on what you want.
- How to brainstorm the facts.
- Mind storming is not brainstorming.
- Speed up your reading to create more time.
- The key facts of applying the 80/20 rule.

- How to use the relaxed creative brain states.
- Why you need to keep a pad with you.

By using these skills, you will have extra time to research and extra information to increase your performance.

Stay open minded, as in these fast-changing times skills that appear slightly outside the norm can be the ones that make us more effective, more smart and more efficient.

> **T!P TOP TIP!**
> The real skill is to use whole-brain thinking, using both the left and right side – the left and right hemispheres – so you can see opportunities when they occur, think about the opportunities overnight, read the signals and signs and negotiate a better deal.

I realised very early in my negotiation career that we have to get a real handle on everything we are negotiating, all the different people that we are negotiating with and their emotions and drivers. By doing this, it helps us see all angles and also where the other person is coming from.

Good negotiators have to be reasonably competitive or they put themselves into a competitive position while they are negotiating. Whilst the outcome we want is win win win, we have to have all the resources at our finger tips to be aware of everything that is going on.

The more we can learn about the emotional and the logical side of where people are coming from, the more effective we will be.

Early on, I was pointed in the direction of how the brain works. I enrolled in a course run by Tony Buzan, who had had a very successful television series called *Use Your Head*. It still gets a lot of views on YouTube (see www.youtube.com/watch?v=LnYVJKxyRPM).

Subsequently, Buzan went on to write many books on the subject of mind mapping and the benefits.

However, Buzan wrote about studies into the brain showing that it is a very complex organ that continues to surprise the neuroscientists and experts as new discoveries are made.

Whole-brain thinking and how it can help us as negotiators

Background

In the 1980s, Roger Sperry and Robert Ornstein, Californian neurosurgeons, received a Nobel prize for the pioneering work they did on brainwaves and the specialist functions of our brains. The work has carried on and the understanding of the brain has grown immensely from what was a very low base at the beginning of the 1970s.

> *There is a view that we still understand and use only around 10 per cent of our brain's capacity.*

What Sperry and Ornstein found was that the two sides of the brain were linked by what is known as the corpus callosum, which is a vast number of nerve fibres, said to be up to 200 miles' length of wiring.

> **T!P TOP TIP!**
> We have two sides to our brain: left and right. Learn how to maximise both to find more solutions and have more effective negotiating results.

Two brains? The two sides of the brain, which often are known as the left side and the right side engage in different activities.

The left side of the brain processes logic, reading, writing, words, analysis, reason, linear activity, the type of work linked to exams, schools and qualifications, the academic type of work.

The right side of the brain processes imagination, colours, visual information (reading body language and signals), spatial awareness, seeing the big picture rather than detail, emotions (emotional intelligence) and intuition (gut feel).

While the left brain is engaged in analysis, the right brain is more connected to alpha wave or a calm state, which I will explain later.

What does this mean for us as negotiators?

For our purposes, when we are negotiating and preparing ourselves for the negotiating meetings, it is very helpful to use both sides of the brain.

Figure 10.1 Left and right brain functions

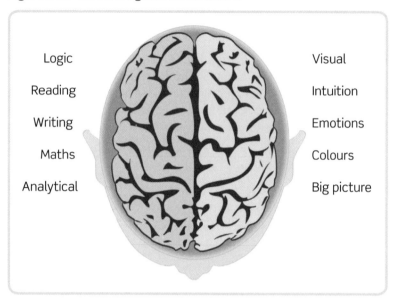

Logic	Visual
Reading	Intuition
Writing	Emotions
Maths	Colours
Analytical	Big picture

For example, a great deal of the preparation will be left brained: analysing, researching, preparing spreadsheets, costings, reading, writing, asking for information via email, examining LinkedIn profiles for information about the other side.

However, when we get to the negotiating table and further down the negotiating process, many right brain functions come into play: reading the visual information, the body language, listening to the voice tonality, seeing the big picture, watching the emotions, working out whether people are telling us the truth, trusting our gut feeling and testing that against the facts as we know them and then rechecking the facts.

THE BRAIN USES A LOT OF ENERGY
The brain does use a lot of energy, approximately 20 per cent of the energy our body uses, which is why, when we are doing a lot of thinking or are in a big negotiation, we can get quiet tired.

So we need energy, breaks and time to talk with our colleagues to discuss what we have all seen, heard and felt.

Conscious and unconscious mind

It said that the conscious mind can hold only seven – plus or minus two – things in the head at the same time. Everything else is stored in our unconscious mind.

Apparently, we never forget anything; it is all there, it is just a case of remembering it. Recall is the problem.

We tend to notice many things, even though our brain has to filter many things out, just to keep us sane and prevent us from suffering overload.

One of the reasons we know the unconscious brain stores all our experiences is that, when an event triggers a thought, we can, quite often, recall something in the past in vivid detail. The higher the emotions at the time of the experience, the more likely something will trigger off the memory.

Memory is linked to emotional experiences, which anchor them in parts of our brain that store information.

Music is a very powerful trigger. If a piece of music was playing when we had a huge emotional experience, something really good or something really bad, the experience can be anchored to the piece of music. That is why, when the piece of music next plays, we remember the incident, the person or the experience.

Why do we have filters in our brains and how can we use these filters to our advantage?

We are bombarded by so much information during our waking hours. It is impossible to take everything in. If we did, we would be so overloaded with information that our brain might stop taking anything in.

Our brain has filters to avoid us having too much information. The filters tend to delete, generalise or distort information. This is why people miss many things that others see or hear. When we go to watch a show or a sports match, very often the person we go with will notice things that we do not.

Digital dyslexia

The psychologists now are calling information overload digital dyslexia. This refers mainly to the amount of email, digital information that we receive and appear to need to read. We need to apply the 80/20 rule and practise our skills in this area (see below).

So, how do we use this to our advantage when negotiating?

Pay attention to what you might be missing

Try this experiment.

> How many Fs can you count in this sentence?
>
> *Finished files are the result of years*
>
> *of scientific study after years of practical application.*

Even though there is no trick here, people get different answers. Some people only see three, five or six Fs.

This shows that vital information, which is staring us in the face, often is missed. In this exercise, some people speed read and miss the Fs in the ofs, others do not pay attention.

If we cannot see the number of Fs or we cannot see the gorilla below, we need to train ourselves to be more observant: observing the things that are going on around us and what the other side might be saying, doing or communicating through silent signals.

(There are seven Fs in the sentence above.)

The invisible gorilla

There is a book written by Dr Richard Wiseman, a UK psychologist, called *Did You Spot The Gorilla?*. The title is based on a piece of research conducted at the Harvard Business School by psychologist Dr David Simons.

A video clip is shown to the audience in which two teams of basketball players are passing the basketball to each other. Why not take a look at it on YouTube (http://www.youtube.com/watch?v=IGQmdoK_ZfY)?

The audience is asked to count the number of times one of the teams passes the ball. Because they focus on this, the majority of people do not notice a person in a gorilla suit walk across the screen. It is amazing.

Many people have seen the clip, as it has been shown on television around the world and played on the internet. Many of the people who have seen it before still fail to see the gorilla.

> *This phenomenon is called inattentional blindness. It is very important in a negotiation to be able to focus on everything that is happening and is being said so that we do not miss the gorilla.*

(For a copy of the DVD, go to www.viscog.com.)

The reason for missing the *gorilla* is that people are so busy focusing on something else, counting the passes, that they fail to notice the distraction.

This happens in real life and particularly in negotiations. People become so focused on the deal that they miss all the other information that is available that might make them change their mind, change the price or change the terms and conditions.

You might miss the intonation, the body language, the personal agendas, the feeling that all is not well with their side of the bargain. You need more time to check things out because the other side are too pushy, trying to close the transaction quickly.

Take a little time to raise your awareness of what is going on around you. You will be surprised by the results you will get.

OPPORTUNITYISNOWHERE

Did you see . . . ?

OPPORTUNITY IS NOWHERE

or did you see . . . ?

OPPORTUNITY IS NOW HERE

Train our brain

The issue is that, unless we train or programme our brain to take in what we want to see, hear or feel, we may filter out relevant information, information that is relevant to the goals of our negotiation.

So, in a negotiation, if we want to hear, see and intuit what is going on, we need to either take someone with us or make a special note to watch for these things during the course of the meeting, *consciously*. After a while of consciously doing it, we will start doing it without thinking.

The information comes in through our senses and, for the purpose of our negotiating, the two main senses are seeing and hearing. How you feel about the situation can be important and that is linked to our sixth sense, intuition.

 WARNING!

However intuition works, my advice to you in a negotiation is do not ignore your intuition or gut feeling.

The filters that control the amount of information that goes into our minds are deletion, generalisation and distortion.

Figure 10.2 The filters of the brain

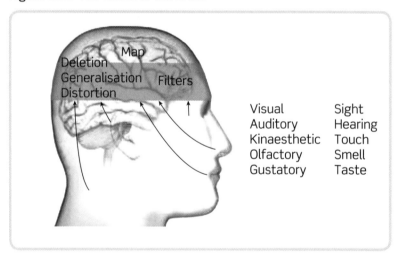

Mind mapping

Mind mapping is a technique I use when preparing for a negotiation. It utilises both sides of the brain.

I use it frequently when I am preparing for a negotiation, when I am in a negotiation and when I am summarising all the key points. It enables me to get all the information on one piece of paper, in a clockwise order and to add extra information easily to the map. I recommend it.

It is a skill that utilises more of our right brain/the unconscious side of the mind, where our creativity resides. The joined-up lines link to each other and move in a clockwise direction. The mind map can include colours and pictures and I find it greatly enhances recall. This is particularly helpful when you are in a tense or stressful state, which a key negotiation can create.

I remember when I was in Liverpool, negotiating with a national retailer, I could not remember how to work my calculator. I exaggerate, but I could not work out how they had switched the numbers round from a per item base to a fixed tariff and how that computed.

Why? Because I was stressed and under pressure. I had been set up in a room, with four members of the retailer's finance department, kept waiting and then intimidated by their various ploys. My mind map helped me quickly focus back on the key issues and the goals of the negotiation from our side.

HOW DO YOU CREATE A MIND MAP?
You start with a plain piece of paper, turned landscape. I prefer A4 because it is a regular size and you can keep it easily available in your files.

Why landscape? Because that makes easier connections with your eyes and your brain. We have two eyes, approximated two inches apart, which means we see images more sharply and more clearly with both eyes open. Widescreen TVs are easier to watch rather than square TVs, which we used to have. Computer screens are wider than they are deep.

Then we start in the middle of the sheet with our subject title, for example, 'The John Lewis negotiation'. We draw lines out from this. I might use these as key lines:

Objectives

Agenda

Research

Key issues

Variables

BP-TP-WAP-AP

USPs

Tactics

Body language

Other business

Reminders

Summary

Handling objections

Follow up

You might decide to use other headings. Under these headings you could have subheadings. You could use small drawings to remind you of key points. You might use colours to make the mind map more interesting. Interest stimulates memory.

When you have finished the first draft, put it away and wait until you remember other points that you can add after you have slept on it (see the alpha state section later in this chapter).

Here is an example of a mind map on body language.

Figure 10.3 A mind map on some of the key points in this book

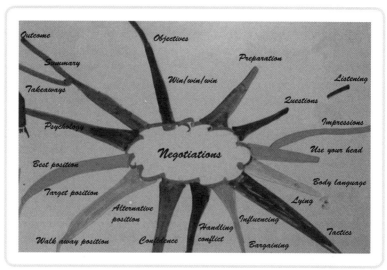

Brainstorming

Another very useful technique for preparing for a negotiation is brainstorming. It utilises the powers of both sides of the brain and the collective ideas of the people who attend the meeting.

HOW DO YOU DO IT?
Invite up to six people to gather together in a room. State the negotiation issue on a flip chart or a large piece of paper in the middle of the room.

Let us say the problem is you have this tricky negotiation coming up with your key client, your biggest and most profitable client. You know you have been making good margins and you are expecting at the renegotiation to have your price reduced.

You appoint a facilitator, whose role is to take all the ideas that come up and write them on flip chart paper.

The rules are:

1. Everything team members suggest is written down.

2. Nothing is rejected.

3. No one assesses or judges anything.

4. However crazy people think the ideas are, no one is allowed to criticise.

The reason there is no judgement is that, if people think others think their idea is crazy, then they and others may not come up with other ideas. Generally, it is the left-brain-analytical people who have the most difficulty not to judge the ideas at this stage.

The pieces of paper are stuck to the walls where everyone can see them.

After a period of 15 minutes, or longer if ideas are coming up, the facilitator stops the process.

I did this with a team I was working with when we were negotiating with a major retailer. We discovered that there were 12 variables that we did for them that we did not know about formerly when we went to the negotiations. We were able to put those into our value proposition and negotiate an extra fee for them (albeit a small fee).

Mind storming

This is, in effect, solo brainstorming. It is a technique where you set yourself a challenge to find 20 points that you need in order to review your research before a negotiation. You pose a question at the top of an A4 piece of paper.

What are the 20 key points I need to think about before we go into this negotiation?

Then you list the points. It is quite easy until you get to around 12 points. That is when it gets difficult. It can be the last eight points where you discover the real issues that you have not thought of.

You should keep going until you have 20 key points.

Smart reading or speed reading

How to double your reading speed and save four and a half days per month in this information overloaded world.

We really have to read faster in order to obtain all the necessary information for a successful negotiation nowadays. Strangely, by doing so, we comprehend more. Yes, that is true, even though it does not sound right.

To negotiate well you have to have all the information at your fingertips. There is no excuse for not reading all the material available.

When I was in San Diego recently, I heard some research statistics, which I found extraordinary. Apparently, the average person now spends approximately three hours per day reading about business-related issues: emails, articles and reports.

That is 90 hours per month. Or 9 days per month in a 10-hour day. So, if you double your reading speed, you will have four and a half days per month extra, for you.

Here is how you do it!

1. Decide you are going to read faster. Mindset – belief.

2. Use your finger to focus your eyes on the words and lines and speed it up.

3. Use your mouse, if you are on a computer, to follow the words.

Using a pointer, your finger or a mouse, is called visual pacing. You are pacing your eyes across the text and learning to cut out all the spaces, gaps and peripheral words that are not important.

How does this help? It helps because, when we read normally, like a normal person, our eyes have to take in the spaces that separate the words. This is unnecessary because our brains are so clever they can blank that out. They know that is a space and not very useful.

So, by using our fingers or our mouse, now we can increase our reading speed by moving more quickly and in a much more flowing movement.

Try this.

EXERCISE

Ask someone to hold up a piece of reading material and watch their eyes move in a jerky formation as they stop between each word. By using a finger or a mouse, almost immediately you double your reading speed. Then, as you get quicker, you will learn to scan down the page in one flowing movement, increasing your speed by perhaps another 50 per cent.

Try this website to test your reading speed: http://www.readingsoft.com. You can also read Tony Buzan's book, The Speed Reading Book (Mind Set) (2009).

Apparently, an average reader reads at 200–240 words per minute, a super-fast reader at 700–1,000 words per minute. I have tested mine on this website and I got to 709 words per minute, but it felt too fast for my level of understanding. I think I can read at around 550 words per minute.

However, in a negotiation situation, really you are skimming for the key material needed. Skimming websites, emails, Excel documents, Word documents, PDFs, etc. to find the key information. Of course, when you find something really important, you mark it up, so you can go back and analyse it properly.

Photo reading

Some people are able to photo read. I have never tried it myself, but have been interested in it. It is another name for being able to turn pages and take all the information in very, very quickly.

If you are interested in learning to photo read, here is a link to a clip about photo reading: https://www.youtube.com/watch?v=yLklT6NoDnU.

The 80/20 rule and why it is so important

Vilfredo Pareto was a nineteenth-century Italian economist. He noticed that 80 per cent of the property and 80 per cent of the wealth was in the hands of 20 per cent of the people. As he was an economist, he became interested in how this might apply to business and life.

He discovered that this rule, or law, seemed to apply to everything we do.

> 80 per cent of the profits come from 20 per cent of the customers.
>
> 80 per cent of the key numbers are contained in 20 per cent of the figures.
>
> 80 per cent of what you need to know in a negotiation is contained in 20 per cent of the information.
>
> 80 per cent of the key points in a negotiating meeting are contained in 20 per cent of the time.
>
> 80 per cent of the meaning in a letter, or an email, is contained in 20 per cent of the words.
>
> 80 per cent of the concessions in a negotiation come in the last 20 per cent of a negotiation.
>
> 80 per cent of negotiated agreements come in the last 20 per cent of the time available.

How does this affect our negotiating? In many ways, once we understand this and focus on it in our everyday negotiations, it will make us much more productive and give us a competitive edge.

If the first letter of a word and the last letter of a word are correct, usually we can understand the meaning. This shows how clever the brain is and how much extra we can get done – researched in our negotiations when we go for it.

How to use creative ideas to solve a negotiating impasse

How to access alpha and theta states

BACKGROUND
Electrical activity coming from the brain is shown in the form of brainwaves on the various pieces of measuring instruments. Typically, this is called an electroencephalograph.

Beta state
When the brain is aroused, like mine is at the present time whilst writing this book, it generates what is called beta waves. The beta waves are the fastest of the four brainwaves that were described first by Hans Berger in 1926. The frequency of beta waves varies from 15–40 cycles per second. A strong connected mind is a characteristic of beta, an active conversation, giving a talk or a presentation.

Alpha state
The next form of brainwave activity is alpha state. This is a condition of relaxed, peaceful wakefulness, devoid of concentration and sensory stimulation. It is characterised by alpha waves at a frequency of 8–13 Hz (as recorded by Hans Berger, a German neurologist, best known as the inventor of electroencephalography, the recording of brain waves, in 1924) and is accompanied by feelings of tranquillity

and a lack of tension and anxiety. Biofeedback training and meditation techniques can be used to achieve this state.

It is suggested that in this state we get our best ideas – the solutions to issues we have been labouring on at work, around the negotiating table. Often these ideas come to us when we wake up in the middle of the night, just as we are drifting off to sleep, just waking up, or perhaps simply relaxing.

Some people get ideas when they are least expecting them – when driving their car, sitting on a train or in the gym. Wherever you are, it will happen to you.

> **T!P TOP TIP!**
> Do not forget to have a notepad with you to record your ideas.

Generally, these ideas disappear within 10 seconds, so it is a good idea to write them down straight away.

A person who takes a break from a negotiating meeting and has a walk in a garden or just takes time to reflect is likely to be in alpha state.

Theta state
Theta is the next state. This is of a lower frequency. A person who has taken time off from a task and begins to daydream is in theta.

If you find you are driving on a motorway and you cannot recall the last 20 minutes, that is often theta state. The monotony of driving on a motorway compared with the concentration on a minor road (beta state) would differentiate the two.

That is why usually I carry a recording device with me when I am on a long journey so, when I do get ideas, I can record them immediately. I remember the PA to the chairman of Barclays saying she used to wake up in the middle of the night with things she had to do the next day and she always used to phone herself and leave a message on her answerphone. If I did not have a notepad, this is what I would do, on my hands-free phone, to the answerphone on my mobile.

It is suggested that between alpha and theta might be the place where we get those Eureka moments that Einstein described in his description of how he found the law of relativity: deeper sleep.

Delta

As a matter of interest, the final brainwave is delta. This is the slowest frequency, a deep, dreamless sleep at the lowest frequency.

Below delta is the state where you have no worries whatsoever. If there are no brainwaves, you are dead, and therefore there is nothing left to negotiate.

> **T!P TOP TIP!**
>
> Keep a pad, notebook or an electronic recording mechanism with you at all times. Creative ideas come when you least expect them.

Sleep on it

It is really strange, but, when I first heard about this, I wondered about it.

I read that Paul McCartney kept a notepad by his bed and woke up in the middle of the night with a tune in his head. He called it scrambled eggs and he thought it was an old jazz tune his dad used to play. He ran it past John Lennon and they changed the name and the words to 'Yesterday'. 'Yesterday' has been one of the best played and highest earning songs over the last 50 years.

Similarly, Keith Richard of the Rolling Stones intuitively knew that when he had ah-ha! moments, he needed to capture them. He kept a recording device near where he slept and, one day, woke up out of a light sleep (alpha state) with the chords of 'Satisfaction' in his head.

Sleep on it has two advantages:

1. It gives you a clear chance to access your alpha/theta mind.
2. It avoids you saying something on the spur of the moment that you might regret.

I have heard of two other ways of accessing your creativity:

1. Lie down and roll your eyes up.
2. Put your tongue into the roof of your mouth.

As I tested learning how to do this, I was attending a speaker's convention in Fort Myers in Florida. Whilst there, I visited Thomas Edison's summerhouse, where he got many of his creative ideas. Edison used to take a catnap five times a day, whereby he laid down flat and created that alpha/theta state where creativity seems to come out the blue. He recorded all the ideas in his books and notepads, as he knew one had to record all ideas when they came.

Edison, when challenged that he was probably crazy and would never invent a lightbulb that worked off electricity, said: 'I have found 1,000 ways of not inventing the lightbulb; I am 1,000 ways closer to my goal.'

As an aside, Henry Ford built his summer house next door to Edison so that he could learn from the great inventor. Some would call it modelling the thinking patterns. Edison still has almost more patents registered to his name than anyone else in the world.

Ford was told that a black mass-produced car would never sell and the quote he is most famous for is, 'Whether you think you can or whether you think you can't, you are probably right.'

EMOTICONS

A picture paints a thousand words.

Today, so many people are using emails and instant messaging. The use of emoticons behind a statement can help to soften the statement. We need a better price ☺ softens the request that looks a little bland on its own. Research shows that how the receiver is feeling dictates how they respond or react to an email.

As emails are one-way communication, we cannot check the tonality or the body language with the other person before we respond, so we run the risk of misunderstandings.

With the send button between you and a misunderstanding, it is better to stop and check your emails. If you compose an email to a client in a negotiating situation, I would recommend some safeguards:

1. You address the draft to yourself, in case you press the send button by mistake.

2. You print it out and read it through carefully before you send it. Many people find it easier to understand how it will look to the other side when it is printed.

Now my professional clients are saying to me, 'Derek. It is unprofessional to use emoticons.' I am challenging them back and asking, 'Is it?' The times are changing fast. Communication is changing fast. It is vitally important that the other side understands the issues and it is framed in the best way. If the odd emoticon helps in email format, then it helps. After all, we used to meet people face to face, telephone them or write them letters where we had more time to consider the outcomes than we do these days with instant mail. However in a legal context or a contract perspective when email is being used for that purpose, they should be avoided.

Margaret Thatcher: A New Illusion

SOURCE: THOMPSON, P., 'MARGARET THATCHER: A NEW ILLUSION', *PERCEPTION*, 1980, 9, 483–4.

This figure shows how the brain distorts and sorts information that might not be right.

When we are negotiating, we need all the information possible. In this picture, the artist has reversed the eyes and mouth of Margaret Thatcher. However, upside down, it looks normal. Turn it round and see how strange it looks.

When you are negotiating and you are keen to get a deal, it can be easy to see what you want to see rather than the totality of the transaction you are negotiating.

Recap

- Improving your knowledge and skills in these areas will help you with getting better negotiating results.

- Watch things that are happening around you; it will improve your negotiating.

- Switch your sensory acuity on, your 'radar', your intuition.

- Fast track business efficiency skills using your brain, such as 80/20, speed reading and mind mapping, to help you with your preparation and your negotiating results.

11.
Read body language

In this chapter you will learn:

- Why it is important to read body language when negotiating.

- How to spot many of the silent signals, the signs that will give you an insight into what people are thinking.

- How to manage your own body language so as to create the right impression and give positive signals to the other side.

- How to make better negotiating judgements: by being more familiar with what the body language signals usually mean.

Introduction

Reading body language is crucial for making decisions when you are negotiating.

T!P TOP TIP!

Reading body language can be intuitive and common sense. The problem with common sense is that it is not that common.

Body language helps us to understand what people are thinking and what they really mean by reading their gestures. It is not difficult to read body language, but people tend to ignore it and rely on what is said.

You will note that, generally, reading body language is a skill that needs to be observed consciously.

Reading body language generally is a right brain skill. Whilst our unconscious mind is pretty good at picking up the signals, it is more likely that they will be ignored because we are concentrating on numbers, figures, listening, thinking what to say next and working things out in general.

It is vital in a negotiation that we observe, interpret and check the non-verbal signals we are receiving to ensure they match the verbal evidence. The body and the mind are inseparable; how we think shows somewhere in our physical micro-expressions (small, usually facial, expressions that we would not consciously see).

The drunk in a bar says:

'My dog plays poker.'

The barman asks:

'Is he any good?'

The drunk says:

'No – he is hopeless. Every time he gets a good hand, he wags his tail.'

The moral of the story is:

Do you wag your tail in a negotiation – or do you play your cards close to your chest?

Original research into body language

The original research into the impact of communication skills shows the following breakdown of how we receive or interpret the information:

Only 7 per cent comes from the *words*: *what* is actually said.

With 38 per cent from the *tone of voice*: the *way* it is said.

And 55 per cent from the *silent speech signals*: the *body language*.

There have been a lot of different calculations for this since; however, you will find that most books quote these figures.

Personally, I do not mind because originally they showed how important body language was to what is going on and, even if we now accept that the words have a lot more significance than 7 per cent, body language is still very important.

Therefore, in a delicate crucial negotiating situation, more than half the information available will be visual rather than verbal. We stand a much higher chance of not being misled by watching the signals.

It has been said that only one person in a hundred is proficient at reading and interpreting body language. Yet an *enormous* amount of information we receive comes from sources other than actual words.

> **T!P TOP TIP!**
> Body language signals generally are not noticed consciously, unless we have trained ourselves or we make a conscious attempt to notice them.

If you raise your conscious awareness and look for tell-tale signals, you will become a much better negotiator.

Why body language signals are ignored in a negotiation

- There is so much information that we filter the visuals.
- We find it easier to concentrate on the left brain logical skills of the words.
- We get anxious/stressed during the discussions, which makes us tense and we do not use our right brain observation skills that interpret visual information.
- We are lazy.
- We do not put enough importance on reading and interpreting the way the information is put across.

How to read body language

One signal on its own can be very misleading; it is the clusters that must be interpreted. For example, someone with folded arms does not mean, necessarily, that they are defensive. They might look defensive to other people. However, it might mean they are cold or they are thinking about something else entirely different to the negotiation, and thinking about it negatively.

I knew a customer who normally was very friendly towards my client. However, at one particular meeting, he spent the whole time with his arms crossed, looking very defensive and unengaged.

We called him afterwards and asked whether we had done something wrong at the meeting, something to upset him because, if we had, we were very sorry. 'No,' he answered, slightly embarrassed. 'I had just negotiated my annual appraisal with my boss and he had given me a D report. I was furious and I couldn't help thinking about it.'

 WARNING!
Body language reflects what the person is thinking rather than what they are saying.

Crossed arms could mean the person:

- is cold
- is defensive
- didn't like what they were hearing
- was thinking about something negative totally unrelated to the negotiation
- is not feeling very well.

What is important are the clusters that happen within a short time of a person saying something, asking a question or making a statement.

The important thing is to look for clusters of signals.

In the example above, the folded arms did not indicate a defensive gesture or a negative feeling towards the negotiation. It was something outside the meeting.

However, if we ask a question such as 'Will you be going ahead?' and at that point the client moves back and folds their arms that is fairly certain to be a negative gesture towards the deal.

If this was the case, as wise negotiators, we might pick this up and either change tack or gently challenge the response, depending on the circumstances.

Body language needs to be interpreted in clusters, based on combinations of the following:

- personal appearance
- eye contact and movement
- facial expressions
- hands, arms, legs and other body gestures
- bodily posture
- spatial situation.

We have covered some aspects of personal appearance in Chapter 7 Give a great first impression. However, there are a few issues that are worth mentioning here:

Grooming/dress – you are going to be perceived as a more professional negotiator and have more power the better you look. Like it or not, that is the way the world works.

Facial hair – men with facial hair, beards and moustaches are more likely to be perceived as less trustworthy than men who are clean shaven. Therefore, it might be easier to get a negotiated agreement with people who are clean shaven.

However, in some parts of the world, it is normal for men to grow their hair long and have a beard. So, we have to be careful with cultural norms.

Hair – a smart, tidy hair cut sharp for men and a smart hair do for women is a good start.

General appearance – fingernails, accessories and jewellery should be kept smart and to the point. Modern jewellery or tattoos should be avoided or covered up, as they might not be perceived as you would want.

Posture

Leaning forward

Leaning forward is a sign of interest in what you are saying, what you are proposing in the negotiation. Judge their level of interest and be careful not to say too much, if you think they are about to agree with your proposal. You might ask, 'Is there anything else you need to know?'

Leaning back

Leaning back is a sign of general disinterest in your proposal to solve the outstanding negotiation issues. Match their body language, lean back yourself and try to reconnect with them, to find out what issues they are disagreeing with.

Head tilting

This signifies listening attentively. Watch the way animals do it. They do it when they are listening to what you are saying, particularly cats and dogs.

Tilting your head, together with a warm smile and good eye contact, will increase the impact and build rapport. Use the same gesture whenever you are asking for help or cooperation.

The more rapport you have in a negotiation, the more likely it is that you will be able to ask more difficult questions and therefore get better answers.

Leaning on an elbow

Leaning on an elbow with your head in your hand signifies boredom. The more the head leans on the hand appears to signify a greater level of boredom.

Take care in a negotiation. If you look bored, the other side will perceive disinterest and are more likely to assume that it will be difficult to get agreement with you.

Hands and feet

Hands on the table

Placing hands on the table is a sign of openness and friendliness. It shows that the person is quite relaxed and open minded. When people do this, generally, their palms are open, unless they are holding a pen or something similar.

Open palms communicate honesty and openness. Politicians use this technique all the time.

Steepling

This is a gesture where the finger tips touch and the palms are apart. Making a gesture like a church steeple gives an air of confidence. Be careful when you are negotiating with someone who uses this gesture. Question them and find out why they are so confident. Is it real or false? Poker players often use this gesture to signify whether or not they have a good hand.

The end of a negotiation can be very much like poker: when time is short and you still do not know what cards or tricks the other side has got up their sleeve.

The more information you have, the better informed you are and the better your decision making will be.

Hands pressed together

Hands pressed together, rather than steepled, will make you look like you are praying.

People who do this might be looking for help to solve the problem (perhaps from a divine source) so, if you press your hands together, that is the impression you will give.

In a negotiation, often the signal will be lower than it would be in say a religious ceremony, as the person subconsciously does not want you to see their difficulty. For example, instead of hands pressed together level with the chest, they might be pressed together under the table.

Folded arms

As we mentioned earlier, folded arms can be perceived as a defensive gesture. It could be that the person is being defensive because they are cold, they are having negative internal thoughts, or they are being negative with you. If you cross your arms, you need to be aware of the negative vibes you are giving out. *If you want to be seen as open, then avoid folded arms.*

Folded ankles

The crossing of ankles is also a defensive gesture. It is not as obvious as crossed arms but, potentially, it indicates the same negativity. I read once that people with crossed ankles still have concessions to give in a negotiation. Since then, I have been watching and videoing people in role-plays. It is right: 95 per cent of people with concessions still to give have crossed ankles.

Although I have to say that it is difficult to see their crossed ankles under the table normally, unless you have a glass table.

Crossed legs

Similar to crossed ankles, this is a defensive gesture.

Rubbing the back of your neck

This implies that either the person or the situation is giving them a pain in the neck.

TIP TOP TIP!

'You are a pain in the neck!' 'You are a blinking liar!' These old expressions, passed down through the centuries, were passed down for a reason.

Head/hair grooming

The person you are negotiating with raises their arm and smooths down their hair. In adults, this is a gesture that suggests not knowing what to do next.

Stroking chin

Stroking your chin suggests that you are evaluating the situation or circumstances.

In a negotiation, if the customer is stroking their chin, stay quiet and wait to see what happens next. Never try to sway their evaluation process.

If they lean forward with an open posture, you have convinced them. If they move back and cross their arms, you have further work to do.

At this point, you might mirror their body language, as you find out what their objection is.

Protecting throat/Adam's apple

The throat is the second part of our body that we protect, particularly our Adam's apple. When people are protecting it, and this is a commonly seen gesture, they feel they are under threat. I have seen this many times in many negotiations. We need to find out if the threat is from us or from the fact that if they sign the deal they are going to have problems with their colleagues. If it is the latter and we find out, we might offer them time out to make the appropriate phone calls.

Hands hidden

If we cannot see someone's hands (for example, they are behind their back or under the table), the immediate reaction is to be cautious. Do they have something to hide? In a more dangerous situation, we might wonder if they have a weapon, a gun or a knife. I have been in a negotiation that was very aggressive and it did cross my mind that I could be at risk of physical harm. The person, went red in the face, moved into my space and I noticed they had their hands clenched. I moved backwards very quickly, and looked. They had a pen.

Be careful, if holding a pen. Pointing a pen or waving it around seems to be something people often do without realising it can be quite intimidating. Be conscious of what you are doing with pens.

Foot pointing

Feet point to where the person wants to go next. So, if you are standing up negotiating with someone and their foot, or feet, are pointing towards the door, you know they are thinking about leaving. You have not got a lot of time or you are not holding their interest enough.

Facial gestures

Smiles

Genuine smiles come from the top half of the face. Insincere smiles come from the bottom half of the face.

Relieve your own tension by smiling to yourself when you are on your own before the meeting, not where someone can see you or they might get the wrong impression.

Frowning is tiring, as it uses around 72 muscles, but smiling uses approximately only 14 muscles.

In a tense negotiation, humour, if and when appropriate, can break deadlocks and impasses. However, it must be used appropriately and with the right timing. If not, it could backfire badly.

Watch and listen to funny films and plays. People who are depressed or ill can feel better and recover more quickly by doing so. A smile releases serotonin, a powerful neurotransmitter that makes us feel better.

> **TIP TOP TIP!**
> If you smile at someone they will normally smile back – make someone's day. This is the same as the phenomenon with yawning. If you yawn, generally, other people who you are with will yawn . This is useful for building rapport in a negotiation.

Frowning

This is probably a disagreement gesture, one that often is not noticed enough in a negotiation.

Nodding

Use nodding to get an agreement. By nodding when asking a question or making a statement, you might help the other person to say yes. If they are nodding, you know things are going well.

Head shaking

Notice when someone shakes his or her head. If someone's words are positive, but their head is shaking from side to side, the likelihood is that the words are wrong, and they are in disagreement.

Head down as opposed to looking up

We tell children to look up when they are looking down. Defeated, negative people look down. To be positive and confident, you need to be looking up and then having your head at a 90-degree angle is best, of course.

Eyes: eye contact and eye movements

Keep your eyes open. Use peripheral vision so as not to stare and so you can see what others are doing. Relax your facial muscles, defocus slightly and widen your vision slightly so that you notice things wider than your normal focus.

Eye contact

Holding the right amount of eye contact is important: enough to connect and have rapport, not too much so as to be threatening and not too little, which looks shifty and untrustworthy. With a little practice, you will do this easily in negotiation meetings. It is said that the eyes are the windows of the soul. People connect by making eye contact and therefore a lack of eye contact creates a lack of trust.

Rubbing eyes

We rub our eyes when we are tired and we want to go to sleep. Similarly, we rub our eyes when we do not like what we see.

Glasses

It is important that people can see your eyes, so be careful with reactolite-type glasses and even glasses that have a dark tint. They will make you look less trustworthy to the other person.

Some sales companies have banned their sales people wearing any sort of glasses, as it might hide the pupils just a little.

The types of glasses you wear can make you look more powerful, for example bigger darker rims.

Looking over the top of glasses or taking them off and putting them back on can look powerful.

Visual pacers

Visual pacers are where your finger or an object is used to bring the attention of the other person to an important part of the contract/ the presentation.

Glasses, a pen or a pointer could be used.

You gain eye contact by holding the item up and then moving the item to where you want them to look specifically.

Gaze

Gaze should always be broken downwards. This is intuitive but, if people do not break the gaze downwards, they will look shifty.

> **T!P TOP TIP!**
> When speaking to a group of people, ensure that everyone is included in your gaze.

- *The business negotiator's gaze* – keep your gaze in a triangle between the other person's eyes and just above their nose. This ensures that you are communicating a business message. Holding this gaze gives you control.

- *The social gaze* – when your gaze drops below the other person's eye level, a social atmosphere develops. The social gaze is a triangle between the person's eyes and mouth. This is good for connecting, outside the negotiating room, when rapport has been built.

- *The intimate gaze* – this gaze runs across the eyes and down to the other person's chest *and* even lower! This is not to be used in a business negotiation situation.

> **T!P TOP TIP!**
> Be aware that stress tends to manifest itself at the extremities of the body: our hands and our feet.

Power gestures

Height

Never stand when someone else is sitting, unless it is your intention to dominate or intimidate them. Height is a powerful dominant signal.

Avoid deep armchairs. There was a picture of a famous negotiation where Yasser Arafat, the leader of the Palestinians, was sitting in a high, firm chair and the US ambassador was sitting in a soft, low settee.

Deep armchairs restrict your posture, limit your ability to send out a number of body language signals and make you feel less confident.

Unless you are playing the power game, control your height.

If you are tall and talking to a shorter person, sit down as quickly as possible so that the other person feels equal. I was working with Holly, a tall 31-year-old woman. She negotiated some contracts on behalf of her company with Tesco and Sainsbury's. I asked her how she dealt with her height.

The answer is, of course, use it when you need to and when you need rapport. Make sure you get the other person sitting down with you as soon as possible.

The best height for being equal is eye level: on even terms.

Intimidation

When I was working in loan restructuring after the debt crisis, there was a successful negotiator called Mike. Mike used to get syndicates of banks often to agree, despite lots of misgivings. When chairing meetings, often he used to get up, walk around the room and stand behind people. He told me the other strange thing was that, only occasionally, did people cover up their notes about their negotiating positions that had been agreed internally before they came to all these bank meetings. He used to read them, note them and then use them when he was, as he used to say, 'Banging a few heads together' to get agreement.

Standing up – power/control and confidence

Whenever you need to project confidence before or in a negotiation, stand up or sit up and pull your shoulders back. Alternatively, to feel more confident, stand upright with your shoulders back.

It is impossible to feel down or weak when standing with your head held up. So, even on the telephone, it can be powerful to stand up.

When talking to an important client on the telephone, usually I stand up. You sound more confident.

Space

The power of distance. Invading someone's space could be used as a power gesture. You should respect other people's personal space.

There are approximately four distances when we are considering personal space. Depending on the circumstances of the negotiation, we should respect the other side's space.

Some people might manipulate these distances to increase the speed at which warm and empathetic connections are made. The opposite can be true and authority, power and status can be asserted quickly.

The four distances to consider are:

1. *Intimate zone* – this is 15–45 cm. People guard this zone as if it were their property and let only people they are emotionally close to into it.

2. *Personal zone* – this is 45 cm–1.3 m. This is the distance at which people stand when in conversation by the coffee machine or at parties.

3. *Business/social zone* – this is 1.3–3.7 m. This is the distance at which we stand from strangers, at arm's length.

4. *Public zone* – this *is* over 3 m. This is a comfortable distance from which to address groups.

Male and female

Never stand directly opposite an unknown male. Never stand adjacent to an unknown female.

Approach a woman directly from the front. With a man, start at a more side-on position and work your way round to the front.

Both of these tips will help you get the negotiation off to a better start.

Other significant non-verbal issues to consider in all types of negotiating

Sit at round tables

King Arthur was right: round tables are better because they encourage everyone to work together. They look and feel like we are working together towards a win win win.

Avoid sitting opposite people, as this can look confrontational and win lose.

Only when there is a potential physical attraction between the two parties is sitting opposite each other not confrontational and that is outside the scope of this book, *but* could be an interesting negotiation situation.

Dress up

Remember, you can always dress down, if the other negotiator is more casual than you. However, you can never dress up once you are there.

Once at a meeting, if over-dressed, you can always remove your jacket and roll up your sleeves but, if you are in jeans and a polo top, there is nothing you can do.

Recently, I interviewed two of the top US speakers on a Google conference call (called at the time a Google hangout) from my home office. I chose deliberately to wear a suit and a tie to create the impression I wanted. I knew one of the interviewees would be dressed very smartly and I wanted to be seen as her equal in the dress stakes.

Digging in heels

Often, you can see people grinding their heels into the carpet. That is where this expression comes from.

> **TIP TOP TIP!**
> When you are negotiating on the phone, you need to concentrate 100 per cent to hear the real meaning of what the other person is saying, as there is no available body language to see.

Rapport

People buy from people they like

People are influenced and persuaded by people they like. As body language is 55 per cent of communication, matching visual information is the quickest way to start to get on their wavelength.

Be as like the other person as you can, on the basis you want a win win win negotiated settlement.

Dress similarly, in a businesslike way. Match what they do in a subtle way. Understand their interests and be able to hold a conversation about them.

Isopraxis – Mirror and match or postural echoing

There has been a great deal of work on this subject, ranging from psychology books to research at the Harvard Business Schools and other pre-eminent bodies.

Human tendencies to imitate clothing styles and to pick up the non-verbal mannerisms of others are found in the reptilian brain. Imitation is a deep, reptilian principle of mimicry, i.e., of copying, emulating or aping a behaviour, gesture or accessories, including impulsive tendencies such as clapping when audience members nearby applaud and yawning when others yawn.

Isopraxis is the behaviour of people dressing like their colleagues and adopting the beliefs, customs and mannerisms of the people they admire or feel inferior to.

Appearing, behaving and acting the same way makes it easier to be accepted; looking alike suggests having the same views and it feels safe.

This creates rapport by behaviour feedback subtly matching non-verbal communication, especially voice patterns and eye contact patterns.

On this basis, all human behaviours often are characterised by synchronisation and rhythm. We should use this to our advantage when attempting to set up a win win win negotiation.

Because body language is 55 per cent communication, one of the quickest ways to build rapport is to match or mirror someone else's style. You might also match their voice speed, volume and tonality.

Then we come to matching their language. If people use certain words, then you should use the same words. I was with a client recently and she used the words 'tuned in'. This told me she is an auditory person who likes to use auditory language. So, I repeated back to her that we will get her people tuned in to the best practice in negotiation skills.

T!P TOP T!P!

Watch people discreetly in bars and public places.

Look for people who have good rapport with each other and you will notice that, unconsciously, they are mirroring each other's body language. It works. However, note that it is gentle, unconscious mirroring not mimicking.

Use body talk to positive effect in non-business situations

Check out how you are getting on with a dinner date

Test your rapport by moving your wine glass. When at dinner, move your wine glass from your side of the table over to theirs. Watch how they react to this. If they are bothered about it, you need to work harder at your rapport!

Watch people's pupils

If someone is attracted to you, their pupils dilate up to eight times more. Add that to the wine glass test above and you are doing really well. *On a serious note, a good poker hand, negotiation position or other type of excitement will have the same effect.*

Apparently ladies of the night in the nineteenth century used the drug belladonna, obtained from deadly nightshade, to increase the size of their pupils and make them look more attractive.

There is a drug called pilocarpine that makes your pupils smaller, so that you look more aggressive. Someone once told me they knew a person who used it before they went into a negotiation. I was assured it was true, but found it hard to believe.

In animation, Bambi had large pupils and looked very attractive; the wicked witch had beady little eyes.

Make yourself more or less attractive

You can now buy contact lenses that will make your pupils look bigger, or change your eye colour to bright blue or dark brown.

Avoid a speeding fine

If you should have the misfortune of being stopped by a police officer, this is a tactic that was recommended to me 15 years ago. Get out of your car and go towards the officer, reduce your height and open your palms whilst apologising. It is said that this improves your chances of being let off.

WARNING!

In today's more aggressive age, be careful as police officers might think you going towards them is a threat, rather than a conciliatory gesture asking for forgiveness.

Serving people

Research has shown that waiters, who reduce their height when at a table and touch clients on the elbow when helping select choices from the menu, receive bigger tips.

To sum up:

- *Check for consistency* – look for consistent body talk. If you receive body signals that do not correspond with what is being said, go back and check the information you have received. Deliberately ask a similar question and then see what reaction and additional information you receive.

- *Raise your awareness* – if you get two incongruent messages, you know the real meaning is not the spoken one.

- *Base your judgements on the entire picture* – not on one snapshot. Read the non-verbal signs throughout a conversation and keep your conclusion open until the end.

T!P TOP TIP!
Take an observer with you to watch the body language.

I always recommend taking an observer to an important negotiation with the sole job of watching the body language and getting a gut/intuitive feel of the meeting.

As an observer not involved with the process of negotiation, they are much more able to focus on what they can see and hear around the room. At the break or adjournment, which you must have in order to discuss what you have seen, seek the views of the observer before proceeding. You might be amazed at what they have seen.

How to improve your own body language skills

Improve your own skills by watching people in a coffee shop, on a train, at an airport or in a bar, and see what you pick up intuitively about their conversations. You will be surprised how easy it is when you relax and observe.

Alternatively, turn the sound down on a television programme and watch in silence for 15 minutes. You will be surprised at your level of understanding. Watch politicians with the sound turned down and you will be surprised at what you see.

At the refinancing of a loan deal, the treasurer of a multinational television company was asked to confirm that the company could repay the loan at expiry. As he said it was possible, he rubbed his nose several times.

When people say things that they do not believe are necessarily true, often they get a tingling feeling around the sensitive part of the nose, which they rub unconsciously.

Watch out for nose rubbing. When you see it re-ask the question in a different way before making a decision.

The moral of the story is:

Watch and listen to the answer, before you make your judgement.

How to manage your body language

You need to know how your body language comes across to others in important circumstances. You could be giving away vital information.

Do:

- keep a neutral confident pose
- keep your hands open on the table
- sit up straight
- look interested
- make notes, if you are feeling embarrassed or under pressure.

Do not:

- look disinterested
- look too keen
- look bored
- cross your arms
- check your emails

- fidget
- use disapproving facial expressions
- slouch.

Appear natural by:

- listening
- nodding
- staying open.

Make a note to remain consciously aware of your body language in a negotiation and, after a few meetings, you will do this without reminding yourself, unconsciously.

WARNING!

Researchers have found that it is five times more difficult to disguise what you mean or what you really believe with your body language than it is with your words. This is why professional 'liars', such as politicians and lawyers, have considerable training in concealing their visual gestures.

Power posing – fake it until you make it

You can find a lot of tips and hints on the internet in respect of body language and negotiations.

There is one TED talk (the organisation devoted to spreading ideas, usually in the form of short, powerful talks) that I really do recommend from a Harvard psychologist called Amy Cuddy. She was named a 2014 Young Global Leader by the World Economic Forum.

Due to the impact on the mind and body being almost instantaneous, she has proved that power posing increases confidence levels substantially in just two minutes. Her message is that you can fake it until you make it.

All you do is find a quiet place where no one can see you and put your hands on your hips. In the short space of two minutes, this increases the testosterone levels and decreases the cortisol levels (the positive and negative hormones). Find out more from http://www.ted.com/speakers/amy_cuddy.

T!P TOP TIP!

Sharpen your sense and awaken your awareness. You will notice more relevant information.

> *'In life you can't help the cards you get dealt – but what counts is how you play them.'*
> ALVIN LAW

My friend Alvin Law, a motivational speaker, was born without any arms. His mother took the prescribed morning sickness drug Thalidomide in 1969 (www.alvinlaw.com).

Recap

- The truth is often disguised in the non-verbal signals.

- It is the combination of what is said and the body language clusters that need to be interpreted.

- People watch. Read people on trains, in coffee shops and bars. Just watch them and this will improve your skills.

- If in doubt, the body language messages are more likely to be right than the words.

12.
Watch out for lying

In this chapter you will learn:

- Why spotting gestures of deceit will make you a sharper negotiator.
- Some key guidelines to both visual and verbal deception.
- Some typical questions that you can ask to check the signals you get back, if you are uncomfortable.

Introduction

T!P TOP TIP!
The more information you have to interpret the facts, the better decisions and judgements you can make.

People will lie in negotiations. So, being aware of some of the key signs and signals will make you a better negotiator and help you get better results.

In this chapter we will explore the most common gestures of deceit so that, when you see them or hear them, you are on your guard.

Eyes are a good guide to deception. However, there are many other things we should look out for.

Deception comes in many forms

Recognising the basic signs can be very helpful to your decision making, your time management and your business focus.

When people are lying, uncomfortable or nervous, the stress manifests itself somewhere in their non-verbal signals.

Ethics

People have different ethics and we do not know how they behave until we have done business with them over a period of time.

Some people think it is fair game to lie in negotiations.

Some might call it being economical with the truth. Some, and I have met many, find it hard to believe that people would lie in a negotiation.

WHAT ARE YOUR ETHICS?
Your ethics depend on your background, your conscience, how and where you were brought up and also on your life experiences.

I have been told by some people that you must expect to be told lies when you are doing deals, and it is up to you to find out the truth.

Others would be horrified by this statement. Working out people, situations and reading them correctly is part of the negotiation game.

As we have said before, there are not many rules in business so, as win win win negotiators, we have to make sure that people are being honest with us.

 WARNING!
Be on your guard to check and recheck the information you are being told.

The lies we are interested in are the ones that will make a material difference to our business or life decision in the negotiation process.

We are not talking about small white lies here which make the world go round, such as a little flattery; we are talking about material information that will make a difference to our business decisions: the information that will change our best position (BP), our target position (TP), our walk away position (WAP), and consider our alternative position (AP) (see the chapter on preparation).

It has been reported in the newspapers that some people tell many lies a day, hopefully of the white variety.

How people might lie

According to Jeff Hancock, a Professor in the Department of Communication at Cornell University in Ithaca, New York, the following numbers of people are more likely to lie over these communication channels:

Telephone – 37 per cent

Face to face – 27 per cent

Text – 21 per cent

Email – 14 per cent

This shows us that, whilst lying is more likely on the telephone or face to face, we also have more chance of spotting it, as we can hear or see the potential micro or macro gestures.

If we then ask for confirmation in writing, people are less likely to lie, as they know there is an audit trail.

> **TIP TOP TIP!**
> Spotting deception gestures is very important when negotiating. It helps you make more enquiries and, therefore, make better decisions.

Visual deception

Let us have a look at some common deceit signals. Deceivers and liars give themselves away in many subtle ways. If you check the signals and ask further questions you will make better decisions.

Hands and feet

If they are moving about a lot, being a bit twitchy, that is a sign of nervousness or insincerity. Hands and feet are some of the hardest things to control consciously.

Hand to face gestures

Hand to face gestures can be interpreted as, at best, a sign of discomfort and, at worst, a sign of lying.

 WARNING!

If you notice more hand to face gestures than normal, be on your guard.

Remember Pinocchio.

Pinocchio's nose grew every time he told a lie. When someone feels uncomfortable with what they are saying, the brain appears to send a tingling sensation to the sensitive tissues on the outside of your nose. They tend to rub it. Strangely, the same happens if they think you or someone else in the room is telling lies.

Generally, people are unconscious about rubbing their nose, so it is a good sign to spot. Then ask yourself this question: What has just happened to make them rub their nose? What did they say? What questions did we ask them? What did we say? It can be that they think you are not telling the truth and they rub their nose. Consider this carefully, if it is important in the negotiation.

 WARNING!

Rubbing, specifically the nose and surrounding area, is a classic gesture of deceit.

Hands over the mouth

Like a child, covering up the words that are coming out of their mouth is another classic gesture of deceit that is more likely to be seen in children. A child covers their mouth with their hands to avoid the words physically getting to their parent.

Blinking liar!

An increase in someone's blink rate indicates that they are uncomfortable, tense or just plain lying!

WARNING!

'He's a blinking liar!'

People who are uncomfortable with what they are saying can increase their normal blink rate by up to four times, without knowing.

Self-touching

You may also notice increased self-touching. This can include hand rubbing, pulling or stroking ears, cheeks and eyes.

Rubbing hands

The speed of the hand rub tells you how sincere the person is:

- *Fast rubbing* is a win win situation for both of you.
- *A slow rub* could mean the person has only their own objectives in mind, which is likely to be to your cost.

Deceivers and liars give themselves away in many subtle ways – trust your intuition.

WARNING!

If it seems too good to be true, it probably is too good to be true!

In research undertaken in California, nurses who were told to give patients positive news that was untrue had ten times more hand to face gestures than when they knew they were telling the truth.

LOOK FOR THE TELL-TALE SIGNS

When I first became interested in this subject, I was working for a client in the financial services industry. We asked a broadcasting company whether they could assure us they would have the requisite money to make a repayment to us in six months' time. This was a large payment that we were fairly sure they could not make.

The treasurer assured us that there would not be any problem whatsoever. The problem was that he spent most of the time assuring us and rubbing his nose at the same time. We were pretty certain he could not make the payment at the time, so we changed the terms and conditions. Interestingly, this turned out to be the case.

The moral of the story is:

Always look for the tell-tale signs.

On a takeover bid I was involved in, I was asked to see the chief executive of a company to seek their reassurances that they knew exactly what they were doing taking the company into the hotel leisure sector.

Whilst he assured me they knew exactly what they were doing, his body language (fidgeting) indicated a lot more uncertainty. In this case, his body language was showing his uncertainty and indicating that some of the things about which he had reassured us, were not certain.

Unlike the stereo-typical fast-talking car salesperson that we tend to not trust, the opposite is, in fact, more likely to be true. The person who is attempting to deceive us generally will say less. They will also tend to hold more eye contact than normal.

It is a social norm to believe that liars are shifty and do not hold very much eye contact. Professional liars know this and may hold more eye contact.

It is true that, when lying, children will not make much eye contact, but professional liars, who know we won't trust them if too little eye contact is made, tend to overdo it and look you in the eye for too long.

I was in a meeting with a lawyer who was trying to persuade me on something that I really did not believe. It was strange; he kept giving me long stares, almost as if he wanted to see me nod and agree with him. I felt really uncomfortable and, as I say in this book several times, if something feels uncomfortable, you need to start asking yourself why; it is your intuition giving you that feeling.

Eye accessing cues

Eye accessing cues can also be very helpful when assessing whether people are telling the truth or not. 80 per cent of people look up and to the left when they are accessing something that actually happened in the past.

They look up and to the right when they are imagining an event that might happen in the future or when they are inventing something that did not happen in the past.

The other 20 per cent of people look in the other direction, which is why it is important to establish a person's preference at the beginning.

In the film *The Negotiator*, there is a scene where Kevin Spacey screams, 'I know you are lying because your eyes moved to the right.'

When I am interviewing someone for a client and trying to find out whether they are telling the truth, I will ask a control question first, such as, 'What is your mother's maiden name?' and see which way the eyes move, to know which way they move when they are telling the truth.

Then I ask the question I really want answered and watch the reaction of their eyes.

Many police forces use this as part of their interviewing procedure. However, there is no country at present where this has been introduced as acceptable evidence in a court of law.

These eye movements need to be combined with verbal information to give us a good insight to where the truth lies.

Verbal deception

With verbal deception, the voice/speech rate may slow down and, usually, there will be fewer words said than normal.

It is presumed that the reason for this is that the person has to consider more carefully what they say. Generally, there are more pauses, hesitation, ums and ahs, etc. There tends to be a substantial reduction in the length of reply.

Conversely, there is often an increase in:

- voice pitch
- the number of ums and ahs
- hesitation in answering/delays in responses
- slips and mistakes
- pauses.

You need to calibrate when someone is talking normally so that, when you ask the white-knuckle questions, you can see if there are any differences.

As has already been said, professional liars will have learnt how to handle situations in which they choose not to tell the truth. There tend to be fewer gestures, fewer body movements and, sometimes, more eye contact than you would expect.

I have worked with Professor Richard Wiseman at the University of Hertfordshire and we have also spoken at several conferences together.

His research into lying showed, like many similar studies, that good liars often can fool people with their body language. Whereas, when you cannot see them (you are listening to a recording in sound only), the truth often is easier to detect.

Some years ago, Professor Wiseman won a competition to try an experiment on the BBC's *Tomorrow's World* television programme.

He recorded two interviews, both of which were shown on television (*Tomorrow's World*), played on the radio (BBC Radio One) and the transcript was printed in a newspaper (*The Daily Telegraph*). Journalist Sir Robin Day was asked to lie in one interview and tell the truth in another. The subject was his favourite film. He was also asked to conceal what was, in fact, his favourite film. 72 per cent of the radio audience got the correct film, whereas only 52 per cent of the TV viewers were correct.

The TV viewers were fooled by the deception in the body language. 64 per cent of the newspaper's readers were correct.

Police forces often just listen to audio recordings of interviews as, without the visual distractions, they can form a more accurate picture of what really happened.

Linguistic deception

According to Professor Wiseman, linguistic deception comes in the form of a slowing down of the speech rate. An increase in the voice pitch, together with an increase in ahs, ums, etc. with more slips and mistakes and delays in responses.

> 'A liar should have a good memory.'
> QUINTILIAN, ROMAN ORATOR, AD 35

You can catch out a liar with preparation and research.

Words

Check that the words someone uses today match what you have been told before.

Intuitively, we know when someone is not being entirely honest. People have a habit of being incongruent in some way, which is not picked up consciously.

They leak dishonesty somewhere and our unconscious mind is like a magnet that picks up the information.

> **T!P TOP TIP!**
> Someone once said that the best lie detector is the human brain – trust your instincts.

Polygraphs

As a matter of interest, polygraphs have been used for many years to test lying. They work on the sweat glands, heart rate, blood pressure and a few other bodily functions. However, they are not used as evidence in all, bar a few, places in the world, as they are not considered reliable enough.

However, the best test is to trust your gut feel when you think something is not true, just like Peter Falk, Lieutenant Columbo, used to do in the *Columbo* TV series from 1968–2003.

> **EXERCISE**
> Here is an exercise you can try with a friend or colleague. It is very good for raising your sensory acuity to deception.
>
> Sit down with the other person opposite you. Tell them that you are going to think about someone you like and try to disguise your body language. Then you are going to think about someone you do not like and try to disguise your body language.
>
> See if they can notice the difference. Usually, there will be small micro gestures around the face and eyes, which will be different.
>
> Now, think of these two people several times in different orders and challenge your friend to tell you which one is which, by watching your body language.
>
> Then reverse it, and let them practise on you.

Micro gestures – lie to me

If you are interested in this subject and would like more information, there are many books on the subject. The American television series *Lie to Me*, whilst exaggerated slightly for television, is based on research into micro gestures and the work of Paul Ekman, a professor in psychology (http://www.paulekman.com/lie-to-me/).

Typical questions that might be lied about in negotiating situations

Can you go lower?

Have you gone lower?

Is the other offer a firm one?

Does the other purchaser have cash?

Have they got the bank finance in place?

Have you paid any other speakers more than this? (Typical in my business.)

Can you meet the delivery date?

When you ask these questions, look and listen carefully to the responses you get. It will give you valuable information.

Recap

- Always stay alert to being deceived.

- If it does not feel right, if you think someone has told you a lie, ask them a similar question, rephrased, a couple of minutes later.

- Allowing yourself to be deceived through naivety will mean that your negotiating decisions will not be as good as they could be.

13.
Use the right strategies and tactics

In this chapter you will learn:

- How tactics are ploys that can change the perception of power.
- Typical tactics that are in common usage.
- The need to recognise a tactic before you can defuse it.
- The difference between useful tactics and dirty tactics.
- A number of dirty tactics – and how to handle them.

Introduction

For the purpose of this key chapter, the term *tactics* will include the following terms that people might use:

- strategies
- games
- manoeuvres
- ploys
- gambits.

> *'Tactic – a procedure calculated to gain some end.'*
> OXFORD ENGLISH DICTIONARY

Tactics are merely psychological manoeuvres to reduce your position nearer to your walk away position. Ploys designed to change your perception of power. Games that put you under pressure to reduce your expectations.

They range from just a ploy to get you to make up your mind to, at the other extreme, the totally outrageous and unacceptable. Generally, the latter are called dirty, or unprincipled, tactics.

Whilst I do not condone these dirty tactics at all, you have to be aware of them so that you can recognise them, handle them and defuse them.

Most defusing can be done by recognising the tactics for what they are. Either be clear to the other side that you recognise what they are doing, gently flag it in a corridor meeting or ignore it, but do not get sucked into falling for it.

Recognising a tactic is more than half way to handling it, in my experience. Recognise it for what it is – a play to get you to agree to a lower price or lower value.

Whether you like it or not, human nature will encourage us to employ *strategies* or *tactics* to different degrees. Just consider how children use tactics.

Some people say to me, 'But in a win win win situation, surely that is not necessary?' However, different people do different things differently. Whether it is because of greed, power, poverty, hunger or just self-interest, ploys happen and we have to learn to handle them and sometime encompass them to get the deals done in a win win win format, if we can.

Tactics, generally, are used in every game or competition. A sports coach will advise his players which one to use at which time of the game. A tennis coach will advise her player when to play on the opponent's backhand.

Because negotiation often is considered or thought of as a game or a competition, the subject of tactics tends to come up. If you take a collaborative approach, a problem-solving approach to negotiating, then the issue of aggressive tactics will come up less to achieve what you want. However, there are a number of tactics at the softer end of the spectrum that are worth using to help move the negotiation forward or to close the deal.

Children use tactics

Children use tactics as soon as they can speak to get what they want. So, if they are inbred in our DNA and in human nature, it is an important subject to understand as professional negotiators.

Recently, I once watched a four-year-old girl negotiating with her parents to have an ice cream. We were in Guildford High Street. It was a hot Sunday afternoon. Her parents did not want to buy her an ice cream. It might have been that she had already demanded too much, it might have been that they could not afford it or it might have been that she had not eaten her lunch.

Watching carefully, I noticed that she used a number of negotiating tactics. (I describe some of these later in the chapter, in a business context.)

First, she started screaming that she wanted one (*toys out of the pram* tactic), drawing her plight to the attention of passers-by, who thought she might be being beaten (*embarrassment* tactic). Then I noticed that her father looked more sympathetic than her mother (*divide and rule* tactic).

So she played on that. The mother was threatening her with things the girl did not believe would happen, idle threats it appeared, whilst the father, by now, was fumbling for money to buy an ice cream. The mother was not speaking to the father or the daughter. She walked off in a huff. The father bought the ice cream and the girl had a smirk on her face.

Win lose – or win lose lose. I thought to myself, 'That will happen again and they are going to have a miserable evening tonight.' Out-negotiated by a four-year-old.

Sadly, we can see many business situations and relationship situations that end up in similar ways, because of poor negotiating tactics.

The moral of the story is:

That children are natural negotiators. No one taught them but they have a knack of using tactical moves instinctively. There is a lot we can learn from watching children and their behaviour. Be aware of tactics so that you can recognise them, handle them and defuse them.

Is it trickery?

For some people, the mention of tactics implies trickery. I have worked for many companies who employ engineers or designers. Usually, they do not accept people who would play games to get deals, better prices and lower costs. They went to university and sought a career to create, build and design things, not to be at the 'tacky' end of the contract, as one person said to me.

The problem is that different people have different opinions about what is right or wrong, fair or unfair, ethical or unethical.

> **T!P TOP TIP!**
> A tactic is simply a way of getting what you want, or as close as possible to what you want. And getting the other person to come with you!

It may help to reduce the other person's best position; to get as close as possible to their walk away position. And, in many cases, get them to reassess their walk away position, and lower it, often out of fear of losing the deal, losing the contract or just being beaten in his or her own mind.

Strategies and tactics come in many guises

Some tactics might be considered more ethical than others and some considered more fair than others.

Some of the tactics used in negotiations do have an element of psychological trickery about them. Some of them are downright out of order and in the category of cheating and lying. Whatever tactics we discuss, they all have a consequence. We will have to work with most people again and therefore we have to think carefully, if and when we use tactics or how we challenge tactics.

Some are normal life circumstances that help people make their minds up. Some are moderate and some are what many negotiators call dirty tactics.

People have long memories, especially for situations where they think they have got set up, tricked or have had a fast one pulled on them.

Whatever your tactics, the key thing to remember is you will have to do business with these people again or deal with them later in your life. Sadly, the notion of an eye for an eye lingers on in a typical human's unconscious mind, even if they are mature in their conscious mind.

If you play a trick this time, you had better watch out next time.

Recognising a tactic is important

I would go further than saying that it is important to recognise a tactic; I would say that recognising a tactic is key. My experience tells me that less than 50 per cent of people in a professional negotiation do not realise that a tactic is being played.

I think it would be wrong for me to comment on whether or not you should use any of these tactics. However, you need to be aware that they are used in business and in life. If you do not understand them, recognise them and are unable to handle them, you will be at a strategic disadvantage in achieving the outcomes that you want in most negotiations.

Tactics can be manipulative, and how manipulative depends on how people use them.

Typical common tactics and how to use them

Higher authority (I need to talk to my people)

Many people think it shows weakness to say they cannot make a decision on the spot. Master negotiators know that they must always have *higher authority* in their armoury to use, if necessary.

It is powerful to place the blame on someone else for not being able to agree to a request, because it means you can stay in rapport with the other side. It means that they may alert you to other issues that you have not been aware of.

You can use phrases like, 'I would love to say yes, but the committee will not sign it off, unless you give me something else.' Or 'I cannot justify that to my colleagues.'

Never use the name of someone in your company as the higher authority. Why? Because they might ring them up or they might say they do not want to deal with you, but they want to deal with the decision maker.

The higher authority, generally, is a group of decision makers like the board, the directors, the operations committee, the executive committee, the chairman's committee or the credit committee.

If you are a small company, say it is your business partner or your life partner!

Try combining good guy/bad guy and higher authority to get better deals. For example, 'I would really like to do this for you, but my people will not let me sign the contract yet. What can you do to help me with some concessions to get it through their rigorous processes?' or something similar. Make sure it fits with the way you would normally say things, i.e., in your words.

> **T!P TOP T!P!**
> Use this tactic in a tactful way. Remember – generally, we all have to justify our decisions to someone. Whoever that is is your higher authority.

Good guy – bad guy (good cop/bad cop)

In this example, there are two people in the same meeting on the same side: one person is nice; the other person is aggressive. After a while, the aggressive person leaves temporarily and the nice person says, 'If you can agree to this, this and this, then I may be able to get the other person to agree.'

The police use this good cop/bad cop tactic: 'If you give me the information, I will make sure my colleague backs off and does not charge you with the other offences that he wants to go for.'

In a small business, it might be as simple as one partner saying that their other partner would never agree, then asking what else can be given to get agreement.

In a relationship partnership, it can be used by saying, 'My wife/my partner will go crazy if I pay that much. Is there something you can do to help me?'

In a large business, this might be the relationship/account manager saying to the other side, 'I would really like to do this for you. How can you help me get it through the committee/or the board? What else can you give me to sweeten the deal?'

So, as in the higher authority tactic, the bad guys are the committee, the higher authority.

Often people ask me, isn't this a bit manipulative? They forget that, usually, they are not yet making sufficient profit for their efforts and should try to earn more. This is a good tactic to flush out what the other side might be able to pay, and learn the truth of their position.

> **T!P TOP TIP!**
> Use this tactic only when appropriate.

Time

People who are short of time tend to make more concessions. Generally, 80 per cent of the concessions tend to come in the last 20 per cent of the available negotiating time.

Make sure you are in control of the time, so you do not get pressured to concede on a false time deadline.

> **T!P TOP TIP!**
> Use this tactic to help people make up their minds.

Time outs and breaks

When you want to consider an offer from the other side or things seem to have stalled, do not be afraid to ask for a break.

This break often is called a time out, an adjournment or going to the balcony.

(Going to the balcony is an expression that comes out of the Harvard Research project, when they realised that most negotiators were not stopping to review the situation often enough).

The benefits of taking a time out are threefold:

1. *It gives you thinking time.* When we are under pressure, often we cannot think rationally and creatively.

2. *It tends to take the emotion out of the situation.* It gives a chance for either side to calm down and think back to the goal. It separates the people (the emotions) from (solving) the problem.

3. *It gives you a chance to talk to your colleagues,* who usually will have a different take on the situation. The more minds you have working on the situation, generally the better ideas you will get.

Even if you are on your own, take a few minutes to consider the situation. Write it down on a piece of paper, go through your notes or phone a colleague and talk it through with them. If necessary, adjourn for 24 hours, so that you can sleep on it.

TIP TOP TIP!
Make sure you use this tactic appropriately.

Flinching on the price

In negotiating, flinching is jargon for acting surprised when the other side makes an offer. It comes in all formats, from gentle 'You are joking!' to the more aggressive outrage that some people seem to enjoy.

When someone says, 'It costs X', you might simply squint and draw breath before asking, 'How much?' in an enquiring, surprised tone of voice. It might also come with a scratch of the head, emphasising the visual surprise as well as the verbal surprise.

At the United Nations, during the Cuban missile crisis, President Khrushchev of the Soviet Union deliberately banged his shoe on the table to show his surprise and anger to the United States and the other member nations. When they reviewed the recordings of this incident, they noticed that he had not taken off his shoe. One of his aides had passed a spare shoe to him, just at the point before he expressed his anger. It had been pre-planned.

TIP TOP TIP!
Make sure you use this tactic appropriately.

Observer

An observer can be used to read the body language, the situation and the big picture.

Have someone watch the body language and tell you how they think the other side are going to react when you call a time out.

It is very difficult to discuss, trade or argue and watch people's body language at the same time. Make sure you take someone with you.

When you are under stress or thinking on your feet, the left hemisphere of the brain tends to take over. This is the part of the brain that is focused on logic, numbers and detail.

The right side of the brain, which sees the body language, the nuances and the big picture, does not function so well when you are under pressure. So your observer, who is watching and listening, can pick up key clues by being in a calm alert state.

You then discuss their views at the time out.

> **TIP TOP TIP!**
> Use this tactic when the negotiation is important and you want someone else to help you.

Dumb is smart – the Columbo tactic

This tactic is when you pretend you do not understand. This is to make the other side explain what they are asking *again*. It can be used when you think the other side is not telling you all the truth and you want to get to the bottom of all the facts.

Columbo was the famous detective in the television series *Columbo*, played by the actor Peter Falk, who often used the *dumb is smart* ploy. He never seemed to understand quite what the other side was saying and kept asking questions, which implied he had not been listening or he had been distracted. This meant the other person had to explain themselves again and, by doing this, often gave away extra information, either in what they said or with their body language.

Car dealers often use what they refer to as the 'Columbo close' if a customer is walking out of the showroom, having decided not to buy after a haggle. The dealer might say, 'I do not know what came over me; I had forgotten, but we had an instruction from head office this morning that we can discount this car further. I am so stupid. I totally forgot about it.' or something similar: 'Come back. Sit down and I will see what else I can do for you.'

> ## T!P TOP TIP!
> Use this tactic when you think someone might be trying to pull the wool over your eyes, or you do not believe or cannot understand what they are saying!

Silence

The use of silence after asking a good question is very powerful.

Ask a great question and wait for a response. If you need to help the other side, then do, but leave a silence of a good five seconds or more. However, never forget that your goal is to learn where they are really coming from. So do not let them off the hook. Keep probing and remain silent for their response.

When I was teaching at Henley Business School, a delegate told me about a nine-hour-plus silence that he had been involved in during union negotiations. No one spoke for nine hours and ten minutes, he told me.

I saw a picture from the *Philadelphia Evening Bulletin* in the library at Henley Business School. It described how, in the Korean war peace negotiations, the two sides sat and looked at each other without saying a word, in complete silence, for four and a half hours.

> ## T!P TOP TIP!
> Use this tactic when you have asked a really good question and you want their response.

Parking issues – putting things to one side

Momentum gets things done. Getting stuck on an issue can stall a negotiation. It is much better to get the things we agree on out of the way. Park issues to one side where you have disagreement, and come back to them later. It can be very effective to have agreed eight points and have only two things that you disagree on: 'If we can sort one, can you sort the other?'

If you get stuck on issue number one, say, 'Can we park the issues we cannot agree on yet to one side?' Get the things you can agree on out of the way and come back to others at the end.

> **T!P TOP TIP!**
> Use this tactic when you want to keep the momentum of agreement going!

Softening up

If there is bad news to come, warn people early that it might happen. I mean something such as a price rise or a tax rise; it is a very effective tactic to soften up the other side to the bad news early. Governments often do this by leaking information to see the reaction they get from the public and the best way to play it going forward.

When you have bad news to give out, it is a good idea to tell people that something has to happen because of the poor results or the poor sales. You are not sure what is going to happen, but you are reviewing the situation and you will let people know by a certain date. Now you will have to balance this against the uncertainty that this will create and you may want to keep the time period quite short.

The same applies with price rises. When you are going to have a price rise, it can be effective to flag it, by saying, 'Shortly, we will have to increase prices. At the moment, we are holding prices as they are, even though it is costing us money.'

The effect of this is that people are not surprised when the rise comes in and, often, they are surprised that it was not as much as they were expecting.

Psychologically, the effect is that you avoid the element of surprise and do not get an over-reaction.

Three options

Giving someone three options is using the power of three.

They might think they are making the decision to choose which one of the three options that you have offered.

Generally, people find that the best way of doing this is to put the most attractive option in the middle, with the most expensive one first. This tactic anchors the price high in the mind of the other side. Then, the second option looks cheaper, which is the contrast principle. The third option is a cheaper option with no bells and whistles and no extras, which leaves so many options out, they probably will not want it.

You might think of the options as gold, silver and bronze. It is a nice way to get it into perspective.

Professional advisers

Use advisers when you need them. They add authority.

People who earn their fees from giving advice sometimes can stonewall or be unhelpful in getting a deal. Why is that? It is because they have their own agenda. They might be advising you, as the client, to hold out for a better deal. However, we must always remember that they have their own agenda.

Take care how you negotiate with your professional adviser. Do they have any skin in the game? Are they taking any risks or are you taking the risks while the clock is ticking on their fees? Often these fees, if not negotiated carefully by you, are time-based on an hourly rate.

I do not advise anybody agreeing to that, even though many professionals will claim that is how they do it. Shop around for professional advisers, ones who you like and trust and know what they are doing, who will give you a sensibly negotiated deal for their fees.

If the other side have a professional adviser who is advising them to do something that is not in your interests, perhaps suggest a corridor meeting, between you and the principal on the other side (lead negotiator) and say something like, 'I do not think your people are being helpful in getting a win win win deal done. Shall we take this off line and see if we can get something agreed that will meet our needs? Practically, and then within the legal framework that we are trying to reach?'

Get the agreement, or get paid, before you supply the service

The perceived value of a service disappears once the service/ advice has been given.

When you are providing a high-value, highly skilled service, make sure you get agreement for it, including the price, before you provide the service. I once asked a lawyer for a contract to be drawn up. It was quite a simple one and they sent me the contract and a £300 bill, without discussing the fee. As I had not agreed to it, I sent it back saying that was not what I had in mind nor was the fee.

This is the same with any service where the value is based on knowledge. Once you have handed the knowledge over, it is more difficult to justify the fee.

There is the story of the plumber, who knows there is a blockage in the system. He insists the fee for fixing it is £300. Because of his knowledge, he gets his hammer out and taps once and the blockage is unblocked. The client says, 'Hang on. £300 to tap?' He replies, '£50 for the tap and £250 for the knowledge of knowing where to tap.'

> **T!P TOP TIP!**
> Always agree fees before the work starts.

Write the contract, the notes and the agenda

The person who writes the contract generally controls the situation.

You'll need to take copious notes of exactly what was said and agreed. Unless you do this when the other side comes back with the written contract, they may have inserted a clause or some wording that was not agreed at the time, hoping you will not spot it. It happens and has happened to me.

The same works with writing meeting notes for circulation and agendas. By doing so, it puts you in control and you can make strategic and tactical points in the notes, together with action points, that might not have been discussed.

> **T!P TOP TIP!**
> Always try and write the contract, the minutes and the agenda.

Summarising

Summarising can be a very powerful negotiating tactic, summarising what has been agreed. Writing it out on a flip chart or an A4 pad in the middle of the desk/room.

This has the psychological effect of saying, 'Look what we have agreed, we have made a lot of progress and we have only so much to go'.

This also has the effect of stopping people going back on what has been agreed previously. You are, in effect, drawing a line under what has been agreed and showing the other side that they cannot go back. Strong leadership and a strong facilitator can make this work well.

Location – seating plans – setting you up

Where you negotiate can balance the outcome of the negotiation.

- *at your offices,* where you can set up the room to how you like it
- *at their offices,* where they can set up the room how they like it
- *on neutral ground,* which might be more beneficial in a conflict situation, where you want to balance the perception of power and have the benefit of negotiating on neutral territory.

I have been described often as the Starbucks negotiator or coffee-shop negotiator, as there are certain benefits to a coffee shop, if the negotiation is not highly confidential:

- It is on neutral ground.
- The tables usually are round.
- By buying the coffee, you can use the rules of reciprocity to your advantage (see Chapter 14) and build rapport in a more friendly environment.

The original trading negotiations of the sixteenth century were done often in coffee shops in the City of London. They knew a thing or two about negotiating.

Salami slicing

This is quite similar to the nibbling ploy used by children and adults alike, where the party asks for a number of small concessions over a period of time. If all of them were asked for in one go, they would be refused. Asked for one at a time, it appears that you are giving only one small concession each time.

If you think someone is playing this game, then ask them for all their requirements in one go. Get them on the table, say, 'Is that all?' to stop them coming back again, and then negotiate everything together.

> **T!P TOP TIP!**
> Always try to get all the points on the table before you start agreeing.

Off the record

When you are saying to someone, 'Please, let us have a chat off the record,' you cannot always trust them to keep silent, so, potentially, you are broadcasting the information.

 WARNING!
Trust has to be earned through actions and behaviours, not through what people say.

Often, people will say that they will deny anything that is said, if it got out.

Clearly, this must not be something illegal, although you can see regularly in the press negotiations that have failed, where things have been off the record and have come out, gone to court or been given attention by the popular press. This tactic should be used carefully.

> **T!P TOP TIP!**
> Use this tactic where appropriate, but with your eyes open to the fact it might get leaked.

Hardballing

You hold out for a high price, no matter what the circumstances.

You have to have a fantastic product that everyone wants and you will not make any friends while you do it.

Never forget, people will remember how you behave when you have power and they will not forgive you easily when they get the chance.

> **T!P TOP TIP!**
> Use this tactic only if you have other options for a scarce resource.

Entertainment

Entertainment is a great way of getting to know people and socialising.

It can be very helpful to find out about people. What makes them tick, etc. Small, inexpensive entertainment seems to be acceptable in most parts of the world. In the Middle East, it is essential that you take time to get to know people, accepting their hospitality.

However, when does entertainment go too far and start influencing the decision making of either party? A cup of coffee or a glass of wine, compared with Centre Court tickets for Wimbledon, is slightly different, yet companies entertain people at Wimbledon and various other sports and social venues and it is perfectly acceptable to some.

Different people have different rules and different standards. Many companies have various policies and what might be acceptable in one country might be considered bribery in another. The United Kingdom introduced the Bribery Act 2011 to avoid any misunderstanding.

Whatever you do, make sure you are not tempted to take a gift, which might compromise your integrity or decision making.

> **T!P TOP TIP!**
> Minor personal entertainment is good for getting to know people and building a relationship. Be careful where to draw the line.

'There is no such thing as a free lunch.'
JOHN RUSKIN, 19TH CENTURY ENTREPRENEUR

Roll over

If you are in a position of no power, it can be worth using this tactic.

Admit you have nowhere to go and put yourself at their mercy. This is a much better tactic than trying to argue your position when you are in the wrong. You will be found out, eventually. In those circumstances, most people will cut you a little slack. They will, perhaps, not take you to the cleaners, but they will go easy on you. You have no choice because you have nowhere to go, so appeal to their better nature.

In most cases, they will go softer on you than if you were to keep arguing a weak case.

If you have ever owned a dog, you will know when the dog is in trouble and it knows it has done wrong. It will roll over onto its back and show its private parts, which is human nature's way of saying, 'Go easy on me.'

> **T!P TOP TIP!**
> Use this tactic if you have nowhere to go. When you have no power or no position and you are in a hole.

> **WARNING!**
> If you are in a hole, stop digging.

Relative value

Emphasising the value to the other side of what you are selling.

Conversely, devaluing the value of what they are offering you in return.

When I was in banking, we were competing with many overseas banks who had branches in London. We used to emphasise that, if the company had a major problem, they could talk to the main board of directors and the top people who were headquartered in London. If they were with a German or Japanese bank, they would have to fly a long way to talk face to face to their people. How much was that worth?

T!P TOP TIP!
Use this tactic whenever you can.

Props

There are a number of props that some people use to impress.

Psychologically, these can intimidate, impress or change perceptions. Some of those I have seen are:

1. *The car that someone shows up in.* I have come across a number of people who drive very expensive cars on lease. Thirty years ago, the type of car that really impressed was Rolls Royce. Two customers at a branch of a bank where I worked had a Rolls Royce. I noticed their clients seemed very impressed and gave them extended credit that they did not deserve, considering their financial position. These days, the credit checks would be more thorough and a Rolls probably would make people suspicious. A car like a Maserati, a top of the range Mercedes, BMW or a Ferrari might be used more now.

2. *Pens.* Very expensive pens, leather files, brief cases and accessories. Nothing flashy, just assumingly expensive.

3. *Chauffeur.* There is a professional speaker, Peter, whom I know, who is at the top of his game. Peter hires a chauffeur to take him to speaking engagements and carry his bags into the conference room.
   Does this impress people? Yes, some of the people some of the time.

T!P TOP TIP!
Only use professional dress and extras that state your brand. Be careful of people and accessories that don't feel right.

A friend of mine was selling his business, as he wanted to retire. A firm came along and offered him a lot of money, if he signed a very flimsy contract immediately.

My friend had a number of family issues and he wanted to do a quick deal; the offer was very tempting. The buyer mentioned that their offices were in Gibraltar and that he went to Gibraltar each day on his speed boat. Well, this sounded very feasible to my friend. However, when he did some checking, there were no filed records of the company or the individuals. Nothing seemed to check out, yet, the people came across as very credible. They were pressing for a signed contract, when I was asked to get involved. We had a meeting and I asked a number of very relevant questions. The other side were not happy with my line of questioning, even though they could not answer a single question. Suddenly, one of the parties moved towards me in quite an aggressive way. I thought he had lost it. I called a time out, and spoke to my friend. We discussed what was happening and the meaning of what we were seeing, hearing and feeling.

We decided that we would be calm, quiet and check things out further. Later, we withdrew quietly from the deal.

The company have since filed for administration; they had no substance. It appeared to be similar to a Ponzi (fraudulent) type of deal and many people lost money. A disgruntled investor has set up a website naming the scam.

The moral of the story is:

Use only professional dress and extras that state your brand. Be careful of people and accessories that do not feel right.

Dirty and aggressive tactics and how to handle them

None of these tactics are recommended. However, you need to understand them and deal with them for what they are.

Bullying

Bullies generally are people who fit into the off-the-scale competitive category, under the Thomas-Kilmann Conflict Mode Instrument (a questionnaire that assesses an individual's behaviour in conflict situations – further information can be found in Chapter 16). They are used to getting their own way. They understand only winning, and that means a win for them. They do not care about you and win win is the last thing on their mind. In fact, their mindset is 'win win is for wimps'. Fairness does not come into their vocabulary and they will try anything to get their own way.

They might use tactics such as:

- Questioning your integrity.
- Questioning whether you are telling the truth.
- Questioning whether you know what you are doing.
- Belittling you.
- Keeping you waiting.
- Embarrassing you (like the four-year-old and the ice cream example, mentioned earlier).

Brenda Dean, who was head of the print trade union SOGAT from 1985 to 1991 in the UK, and became Baroness Dean Brenda, told me a story when we were recording a video on negotiating. Robert Maxwell, as a matter of course, used to keep people in a hot, unventilated room until the early hours of the morning. At that stage, he might leave them there, hoping for a deal, and then he would come back many hours later and conclude matters. He would have gone upstairs to his flat, had a sleep and come back when they were exhausted, to close the deal. He knew people do irrational things, when they are tired.

How might you counter this type of tactic? Have a walk away position and leave the meeting, walk out. Do not get sucked into dealing with unscrupulous people like this.

T!P TOP TIP!
Recognise it. Do not be intimidated. Stay cool. Walk out. Cut your losses.

Toys out of the pram

This is an extension of the metaphor of the child who is not getting her own way.

They start ranting, raving and fussing – throwing their toys out of the pram. Children are very good at this and some people keep this knack into adulthood. I have worked for bosses who, if you were not seeing it their way, would throw a wobbler, a tantrum.

The best way to deal with this is to let them rant and do not say anything until they run out of steam. Do not take it personally; insulate yourself from their toxic venom (one method of doing this is to pretend you have some bubble wrap around you, and the anger is bouncing off the bubble wrap and not getting through to you).

This takes a lot of self-control, but is worth it. When they have finished, you might very quietly say, 'So, how can we solve this? Where do we go from here?' Or, even suggest a further meeting, once you have discovered what the issues are.

> **T!P TOP TIP!**
>
> Do not use this ploy. Handle the situation in a cool, professional way.

> **WARNING!**
>
> Do not rise to the bait of insults. Keep calm and carry on!

Acting in anger

Act in anger – do not react in anger. This is an over-stated flinch, which we have already referred to. If someone really winds you up, then pretend how angry you are. In some autobiographies, I have read negotiators using the word furious. Malcolm Walker, the CEO of Iceland, mentions in his recent book *Best Served Cold*, on many occasions, how furious he was with suppliers and how he vented his spleen on them. Was it a tactic?

I worked with a friend of mine, Peter, who was a syndicated loan adviser. On one occasion, a client questioned his integrity in the middle of an all-night negotiating session. Peter stormed out of the room. I followed him to calm him down and keep the negotiations going. I was not sure if he had acted in anger or reacted in anger at the time. He had done it on purpose to get his point across to the other side that they could not make personal insults, if they wanted a deal. After a reasonable time out, the negotiations resumed and the deal was negotiated.

> **T!P TOP TIP!**
> In very exceptional circumstances, this tactic could be a way of handling the situation.

Low balling

Low balling is where an outrageously low offer is made in order to get agreement. This is to lower the other side's expectations of what they will have to pay. Perhaps, also, to flush out the other side's walk away position (WAP) and get an agreement. I heard that this is what happened with the negotiations around rebuilding Wembley Stadium. The low-ball bid was accepted and, later, the contract had to be renegotiated several times.

Recognise the tactic and show your surprise that, clearly, they are not serious.

If they put a low price on the table to you, be careful, as they may have to renegotiate the price up higher at a later date, just to avoid making a loss or going bust.

Lowballing is used frequently on building contracts or other highly competitive contracts where the other side assume they are going to upsell you more profitable extras, once they have the contract and the work has started.

> **T!P TOP TIP!**
> Do not use this tactic. It will come back to haunt you.

Deadlock – stone walling

Deadlock needs breaking. Often, in my masterclasses, this is the biggest issue, when nice people who are not used to the cut-throat style of some people, hit deadlock. Often, this is just a tactic played by the other side to see if you will cave in.

Do not cave in – stand your ground, sit tight and ask, 'What should we do about this? We have a problem, how can we resolve it?' Hold the silence again to hear what they have to say.

If you are still getting nowhere – then you might use a yes tag question (see Chapter 8, Ask the right questions). 'Can we just confirm that we do want a deal, don't we?' See what they say and then, perhaps, suggest a time out for both sides to have a think about how a deal can be reached.

> **T!P TOP TIP!**
> You might say, 'We do want to achieve a win win, don't we?'

You may have to come back with a minor concession or even a major concession (remember to make the concession conditional on what you want from the other side).

Sometimes, you are never going to get a deal and sometimes you have to walk away and look at the alternative position.

> **T!P TOP TIP!**
> Offer ways of breaking the deadlock, as described above.

Megaphone tactic

This is a tactic where information is deliberately released to the media or on social media and gets made public.

This is used, perhaps, where there is a high-profile transaction that gets stuck. So, someone might ask their media adviser to have an off-the-record discussion with a journalist and the journalist publishes information about a negotiation over a Canary Wharf building breakdown or similar.

Jobs are at risk and creditors' debts are at risk because the two sides cannot come to an agreement. Everyone denies they know how the story got into the press, including the leaker. Guess what happens? The pressure of the public perception, the perception of the shareholders and public opinion encourage people to move their position.

Governments often do this when they want to test public opinion. Something gets into the public domain; no one knows how it got there.

For example, the government proposes an increase in taxes to fund new hospitals, to see what happens. If public opinion is negative, when asked, the government denies it is true. If there is opinion in favour of tax rises for health care, it goes ahead. It can happen in smaller issues, where a letter appears in the local paper, or someone posts something deliberately on Twitter.

T!P TOP TIP!
This is not recommended in extreme cases without professional advice.

Bugging and other issues

Some people think that this type of issue does not happen in business negotiations. It certainly will not be a win win. However, I have been in two situations, one in Paris mentioned previously, and one in London where we have been fairly certain that the room we were put in was bugged.

It just felt strange and, funnily enough, the language that one of the parties used was odd. They said, 'We have set up this room for you to have your break-out sessions.' Being a good listener, I was intrigued with the words 'set up'. So, we declined their offer and took a stroll round the block when we had our time outs.

Why would they bug the room? To learn of our negotiating strategy and perhaps what our real WAP was!

I was told once that Robert Maxwell had the lifts in his building bugged. I have no idea whether that was true or not. However, I would advise any negotiator to be careful. If something does not feel right – perhaps it is not. Do not take any chances; things happen.

T!P TOP TIP!
Use of this tactic is not recommended.

Wasting time – bore and snore – police

> *The longer the negotiations go on, the more some people will get worn down.*

The lack of progress and, perhaps, the intransigence of the other side ends up getting them to agree against their better judgement. In fact, when people get tired, they tend to make more irrational decisions and this can be used as a tactic.

In hostage situations, the negotiators often might spin out the negotiations so that the people holding the hostages get tired, hungry and thirsty. Often, the hostage takers are on a high, either an artificial high or an adrenalin high, where they might not behave rationally.

The goal of the hostage negotiators will be to get them off that high into a more rational state, where they see the sense of doing a deal. Nothing will be said to wind them up any more. I once spoke to a police hostage negotiator. He told me he had a pretty boring voice and he was a pretty boring person. He thought that had helped his success rate. As a matter of fact, he did sound boring to me!

T!P TOP TIP!
Use of this tactic is not recommended.

Recap

- Tactics are played to lower your perception of power, to try and get you down to your WAP, or even lower.
- Many tactics, such as higher authority or good guy/bad guy are very useful, if used properly.
- Many people do not know a tactic is being played – even after it has worked to lower their perception of power.
- Negotiators need to understand the psychology of what is happening, and be able to counter.
- By understanding tactics, you will be a more confident negotiator and adviser.

14.
Influence the other side

In this chapter you will learn:

- A number of psychological strategies for influence when negotiating.

- The advantages of employing strategies when you are negotiating.

- How to close the deal early using the commitment strategy.

- How language affects you and the other side.

Introduction

I have always been a massive fan of psychology, what makes people tick. That is why I have always looked carefully at the highest achievers in their fields, the people whose research has and will make a massive difference to others.

Some have been psychologists, like Robert Cialdini; others have been students of psychology and, like me, students of the highest achievers. I have no claim to fame but Richard Bandler, John Grinder, Tony Robbins, Steven Covey and Rob Yeung are just a few that spring to mind.

This is why this chapter is massively important to your negotiations.

Influencing is key to getting a successful win win win outcome.

Influencing is a crucial part of negotiation and we have to use influence to persuade our negotiating partner that it is worth paying the price we are asking, agreeing to our requests or trading concessions to make something, which might be difficult, happen.

Influencing means we are using as many skills and as much information and knowledge at our disposal to get the other side to see the benefits of our proposals.

Therefore, the psychology of influence is very important.

Understanding the work of the social scientists and how it fits into the negotiation process is something that I have studied, taught and practised for many years.

There is a multitude of what we could call psychological negotiating tactics.

Most of these are influencers that work below the average person's level of conscious awareness.

Robert Cialdini is one of the first psychologists to research and really drill down into what works, without us noticing. The six influencing strategies have remained the mainstay of the many books that have been written on the subject of influence and persuasion.

These strategies work best when you use them before you start the negotiation process.

So, they are a key part of your preparation, your positioning and your plans. They can be almost as important as the case you make.

The six strategies are:

1. *Liking*
   Make sure the person likes you. People buy from or are influenced by people they like. The contrary is true: if someone does not like you, they are unlikely to be influenced by you.

2. *Reciprocation*
   Giving something unconditionally for nothing sets up a wish to be reciprocal in the minds of the other people.

3. *Scarcity*
   People tend to want things that are in short supply, or they think they might miss out.

4. *Social proof*
   People want things that other people have, even if sometimes there is no logical reason to have it.

5. *Authority*
   People are more persuaded by people in authority, people who look, sound and give the impression they care, people who have power through their knowledge.

6. *Commitment and consistency*
    If someone agrees to something, it is very hard to go back on it later.

> **TIP TOP TIP!**
> Cialdini says, 'The more of these strategies you can put in place before you attempt to negotiate, influence or persuade, then the more success you are likely to have.'

These strategies work because of the way our brain is wired; it likes and dislikes certain things. These all link back to the survival strategies of our reptilian brain.

If we think about our brain as being part of us, something that connects us to our body unconsciously, then it can be said that:

- It likes people who are nice to us. It likes gifts and free items. It likes things that other people have and have done. It likes experts.

- It does not like owing people favours, going back on something it has agreed to and it does not like people who are very much the opposite to their values.

Let us look at these strategies in more detail.

Strategy 1: Liking

People like people who are like themselves.

How to Win Friends and Influence People by Dale Carnegie was one of the first books on interpersonal psychology and it is a book with a very interesting title. It became an authority on getting on with people. The basic premise was *put yourself in the other person's shoes*. It was one of the first personal development books I read and it has been reprinted over and over again.

It was first written in 1937 and has been revised many times since. When you win friends, it is much easier to influence them.

The basic premise of WII FM comes from what looks like a radio station, but it stands for what is in it for me? – when you put yourself in the other person's shoes and you ask what they want. If you can give them what they want, which is not always what you think they want, generally, you can get what you want.

Our perception of what people want often is not reality. There are nearly seven billion people in the world and everyone has a different finger print and eye retina pattern. Therefore, everyone's perception probably is different. Find out what they want by asking.

WARNING!
Be careful about people exploiting you.

Most people want to say yes to requests from their friends and people they like, people with whom they have a rapport, and this strategy can be exploited by people.

In this book I am not talking about exploiting people; I am talking about negotiating win win win settlements. However, you must be aware that some people will exploit some people, some of the time, using any technique. The more aware you are of these techniques, the better able you are to do your job as negotiator.

The opposite is true as well: generally, people will not be influenced by people they do not like unless they have other power over them, such as status, authority or some unfair power.

So, liking is important in any influencing or negotiating situation, as it will be easier to influence, if the person likes you.

Conversely, if you find yourself liking someone in the short period of time since you first met him or her, it is best to ask yourself whether this relationship is too good to be true. Then stand back and take time out of the negotiation, sleep on it or take some time to consider logically the position you are in. This is one of the basic reasons why you should take time out before you make a negotiating decision.

There are small things that you can do to get people to like you and to enable you to connect with them. They are things that make the world go round and are nice to do. However, it is worth considering if you are being manoeuvred to make quick decisions by these psychological techniques.

Are you and your team liked?

When I was with Barclays Bank, I took my team away for an away day to brainstorm how we could differentiate ourselves from other banks.

We were operating in the large corporate market where one corporate loan that was drawn was the same as another one. It did not matter what bank you got the money from; what mattered was the service, the account director, the efficiency, and that they could deliver what you wanted and you liked and trusted them.

So, having analysed the 150 global accounts we looked after, we realised that just a few of our people did not connect with just a few of the finance directors or the treasurers.

The quick win, which I took away and implemented, was to change around some of the personalities, swapping account directors over to accounts where they were more likely to get on with the different personalities. It had phenomenal results.

Here are some useful tips.

Build rapport

Make a conscious decision to do things that mean the other person will like you. Gently match and mirror the language, voice tonality and body language of the people you want to influence. Do not shout at a quiet person and do not be timid with thick-skinned people. When you feel you are getting on with someone, then you can start to *lead* by subtly changing these behaviours. This is called *pacing* and *leading*.

Flattery

Be subtle, sensible and genuine in your use of praise and people will like you for your positive observations. We tend to like people who like us and do the same types of things as us.

> **T!P TOP T!P!**
> There is an automatic positive reaction to people who compliment us.

Physical attraction

When people are physically attractive, juries tend to be twice as lenient. As 90 per cent of our attractiveness is how we dress, no matter how you feel about your physical shape, if you dress well, groom your hair and look smart, people will be more generous towards you.

Therefore, wear clothes that are similar to the other side, perhaps slightly smarter than the other person, as a general rule. Be like them as much as you can.

I always dress up before I meet someone, dressing above how I think they will dress, just marginally. I can always take off my tie and jacket quickly and reduce my dress to their level, if it is more casual.

Be positive

There is a natural tendency to like people who bring us positive news. Positive people bring positive energy and optimism. Conversely, there is a tendency to dislike people who bring us bad news.

Use positive language. (I have listed some positive language at the end of this chapter.) Check your language; make sure you are using positive influencing language.

Do not shoot the messenger

This phrase comes from the ancient stories about how the messengers who brought good news were praised and the messengers who brought bad news were killed.

I remember working for a boss who used to say, 'I want to know everything that is going on, even the bad news, as soon as possible.' I found out early on that it was not good news to tell him bad news, as I got the blame and the responsibility of sorting it. It was easier to leave it to others and let him find out himself.

I was surprised he made these vital mistakes. However, with his leadership style, he lost goodwill and, therefore, he never knew as much about situations as he should have done.

I have heard the same stories about many autocratic chief executives, when people whose jobs depended on the CEO would never tell them the bad news. This is why some companies get into difficulties because they do not know what is going on in the front line of the sales, because no one wants to tell them.

> 'The work of a good barrister is to make the jury like the defendant.'
> ANDREW HENLEY, BARRISTER

Car selling

In this instance, it is useful to study the work of the very best car sales people. They will spend time befriending you, as this will accelerate the buying process, if the buyer thinks they like you, trust you and believe you.

My wife and I recently went into our local Volkswagen dealer where we had bought a car for our son two years before. The salesman, Paul, remembered both of our names when we walked in, unannounced. How powerful is that? Are we more likely to buy a car from him than someone else, if most other things are equal?

> 'The deepest principle in human nature is the craving to be appreciated.'
> WILLIAM JAMES, 19TH CENTURY PHILOSOPHER

Ivan Pavlov

Pavlov is famous for what we now call classical conditioning. His research of ringing a bell when he gave dogs food was ground breaking. He rang the bell, showed them food, they salivated and ate it.

Then he found they salivated just by ringing the bell. There was no need to show or give them food. This is known as *anchoring in the mind*. Then, when a bell was rung, even if there was no food available, the dogs salivated.

Food and drink seem to be a particular anchor that triggers liking for the person you are eating or drinking with. Again, the social connection of drinking or dining with someone creates a liking link, just like Pavlov 120 years ago.

Tribes – age, religion, politics, social clubs

Group behaviour, such as that at football matches, can be described only as tribal. People tend to like people from their own part of town, their own religion, their own politics, their own sports club. This is the *similarity principle*: I like people who are similar to me.

I was once negotiating with a particularly difficult client at a UK retailer and he was using typical procurement tactics: being aggressive, off hand, implying 'you need me more than I need you', etc. I managed to get him out for a meal and found out that we had both played hockey, albeit at different times, for St Albans Hockey Club. This softened the negotiations and the relationship by quite a large degree. I did not win the business that I wanted at the figure we were trying to negotiate at, but we got on a lot better and we had better negotiations from then on.

Good cop/bad cop

I described this negotiating tactic in Chapter 13 in the psychological tactics section of the book. The reason it works is that the bad cop scares the other side with their aggressive behaviour so that, when the good cop comes in and argues with the bad cop and then is nice to the person on the receiving end of this tactic, it appears that the good cop likes the person and they are someone to trust and latch on to.

WARNING!

People like to say yes to people they know and like. They tend to trust them. Take care – trust has to be proved!

Strategy 2: Reciprocation

If you give things to other people unconditionally, then they will feel they owe you something in return.

This is an unwritten law of human nature, programmed into most people's DNA.

The strange thing is that the value of what you give bears no resemblance to what they might feel they need to give you in return.

A *favour* is just that and it is normal to feel you have to return one.

Gifts of friendship, kindness, small entertainment, remembering birthdays, Christmas cards and anniversaries all count.

Giving someone time when you least have it and listening to their issues can be very valuable.

In your personal interactions with people, the old phrase, 'give and you will receive' really works.

> **T!P TOP TIP!**
> Doing helpful things for people, without asking for or expecting a favour returned, makes them feel they owe you a favour back. This must be done genuinely; if not, most people will see through it immediately.

Hospitality works on exactly the same principle as favours, which is why we have to be careful about accepting hospitality and giving hospitality, which cannot be described as a bribe.

Some companies have a policy that no one is allowed to accept hospitality and, if they do, it must not exceed a certain cash value. I work with National Health Service decision makers/finance people and buyers quite a lot and I know they can accept nothing more than invitations to educational events.

When I was working in financial services, one of my clients used to take people to the hospitality box at a famous football stadium. He found that the people who liked football, and particularly one of the biggest clubs in London, were very grateful for the invitation and would always see my client at a moment's notice, even when they were very busy.

I do not know if my client got more business, but I do know they were looked on favourably when in competition. The reciprocity principle worked.

The cost does not matter.

While writing this book, I had a potential dispute with a client over price. They wanted a conference call. I suggested a face-to-face meeting. They suggested their office. I suggested a bar in Liverpool Street station, as the client goes home from there and I was in London to watch Arsenal play Southampton. We met for 25 minutes. I bought two pints of beer and we resolved the issue in the first ten minutes.

Other examples of reciprocity are free samples in supermarkets and waiters giving sweets after dinner, which tends to lead to higher tips. It is no different in business and is why companies give out free samples.

> 'Give without remembering – receive without forgetting.'
> WILLIAM JAMES, 19TH CENTURY PHILOSOPHER

I read a story about a US car salesman, who allegedly earned more than any other salesman in the USA. He employed a PA to send birthday cards, Christmas cards and anniversary cards to all the customers he had served over 20 years. He got more repeat business than anyone else, as they came back to him out of loyalty.

Strategy 3: Scarcity

> 'People want more of things that are in limited supply.
> Always highlight your unique benefits and exclusive information.'

We have a natural need to want things that are scarce. It is another inbuilt psychological phenomenon, which does not make very much sense.

However, as negotiators we need to be aware of it. What it does is position something we have or they have, as something that is of higher value because it is scarce.

If clients I work with make their services scarce or in demand, then they are perceived to be worth more. It decommoditises the product and makes them worth more in the minds of others.

One of my clients is in the consulting business. They are a niche player. Their ownership structure (they are owned by the employees) means their services can be perceived to be of higher value. They can spend more time with clients, etc. because they do not have to provide a stock market profit statement every six months, reporting to the shareholders rather than themselves as the owners. Their services are scarce.

I have advised them to use this as a unique sales proposition (USP) and part of their value proposition when they pitch for business, make presentations or negotiate.

Here are some examples of scarcity being used in negotiating, business and selling:

- 'Offer available only until Saturday.'

- 'Limited edition' – often used to personalise cars and make them limited editions. Also used in making commemorative porcelain or china.

- 'I have only a few dates left in my diary in the next few months' – used by consultants to keep negotiated fees high, close sales and show that the resource is scarce.

- Classic Disney films used to be released for just three weeks a year at Christmas.

- Concert tickets go on sale and sell out immediately. Suddenly another concert becomes available the next day. Then another . . . The Rolling Stones sold out of tickets at £100 each in no time, for their recent Hyde Park concert in London. This forced people who wanted to go to the concert to pay £200.

> **T!P TOP TIP!**
> In life, opportunities seem more valuable when they are difficult to find.

Strategy 4: Social proof

Other people want what others have got and will do what others have done. So, when you are influencing, if you can show others that what you have is what others want, then you will influence them to negotiate with you for it.

Others have bought it, others have it and others have given to this charity. People follow the lead of people who are like them. So, when you are talking to clients about your products in order to get them to the negotiating table, tell them about the stories of other clients and how they have used your products and services and how they have worked really well.

If you can get references from these clients to show the person you are influencing, it will give you street cred. The printed word is very powerful. If not, ask an existing client if they would be prepared to give a verbal reference or email a testimonial directly to your prospective client to help the negotiation process.

Most people who have had a good business experience will be prepared to give you a testimonial, if you ask them politely and give them a pointer on what you are after.

People are influenced by what other people have done. For example:

- Beggars get more donations when they have some money (but not too much) already in their begging bowl.
- In Starbucks, the tips box usually is pretty full with small coins; people feel they should give their coins because others have.
- TV producers put canned laughter on their shows because it is proven that hearing others laughing encourages more people to laugh.

T!P TOP TIP!

This is a marketing tip linked to negotiation. I am always telling my clients that they have to tell people how busy they are. (For some reason often people think it is a sign of weakness to have too much to do.) They have to put testimonials around their reception areas. They have to have letters from satisfied customers on their websites. In my previous book, *Power Negotiating*, I had three pages of testimonials from people who were delighted to share the experiences and profits they had made, by dealing with me. *People believe what other people say, more than what you say!*

Strategy 5: Authority

'People defer to experts. Expose your expertise.'
ROBERT CIALDINI

Do you look the part? Do you sound the part? Does your company – with its branding, first impressions, the way it handles issues, complaints and crises – come across as one that really knows what it is doing?

We can learn a lot by going into a luxury car showroom and seeing how they position their service and their products. The only thing I would say is that luxury car showrooms do tend to go over the top. However, just have a look and think about how you might be able to increase your potential *authority* in the eyes of the client.

Let us look at cars. I know a number of people who think they show authority by the car they drive.

A BMW 7 series driven by a procurement lady who just wants to win.

A Ferrari parked in the director's parking space at a frozen food company.

> *It appears that many competitive people, particularly men, judge one another on the status of the car they drive.*

Personally, I think that over-the-top cars might give the wrong impression. So the situation and the circumstances are important.

Certainly, if you want to be taken seriously, have that authority. Make sure you have a sensible, perhaps slightly upmarket, car.

How trappings make a difference

I find it interesting that many of the researchers call these items *trappings*. Is this to trap you into believing these people are experts?! Here are some examples that show how *trappings* make a difference:

1. *Certificates of qualifications* – shown in reception rooms.

2. *Letters after people's names* – to show professional qualifications.

3. *Uniforms* – worn by police officers, customs officials, etc.

I saw a guard on my local railway line into London wearing a cap, like a police inspector, when he was checking tickets. It was amazing watching how the travellers deferred to his authority and no one was refusing to pay for tickets. I asked him if it was deliberate or he just liked wearing the cap. He told me he does it deliberately and he has the highest revenue collection of his colleagues. He never gets challenged by the late-night drunks, etc. as they defer to his presumed authority that the cap gives him.

This is why customs officials and security guards in shops have started wearing authoritative uniforms.

The way I use the authority tactic is to dress above the expectations of an audience to whom I am speaking. I can always dress down later to build rapport, if they are casual, by taking off my tie and jacket. However, I can never dress up. I also have my books and DVD programmes on display. Not only to sell them (although this is nice), but to display my authority as an expert in the specialist subject of professional negotiating.

Remember to use your qualifications on business cards, CVs and LinkedIn.

> **T!P TOP TIP!**
>
> Consider how you might improve your positioning to improve your negotiating position and therefore your price, with some or one of these minor, but very effective, techniques!

Mind/body connection authority – placebos

I read that placebos work much better if a doctor administers them with total confidence. This is why the doctor must not know which drug is the placebo or he may just give it away in his non-verbal communication.

Stand up to authority – generally people are not prepared to

Captains of aircraft, ships, war generals, prime ministers and presidents tend to hold so much authority that people are not prepared to argue with them or put forward a different opinion when they know they are wrong.

The risks of too much authority

When a respected captain of an aeroplane with engine problems switched off the wrong engine in a landing at East Midlands airport a number of years ago, the co-pilot noticed the error, but did not stand up to the captain. Aviation authorities now give assertiveness training to co-pilots in order to overcome this bias towards authority.

I once went to a client's office where the reception desk was not manned, no one answered the bell and, when I looked around the area, it was dirty and dusty. That is the worse situation I can remember. I think that, with cost cutting recently, many companies have to be very careful that they do not give the initial wrong impression of their branding and positioning of the products and, therefore, command a lower price than they otherwise might do.

Strategy 6: Commitment and consistency

'People align with their clear commitments.'

When people make their commitments active, public and voluntary, they tend to stick to them because they want to appear consistent.

Get a public commitment from others you are working with by using phrases like, 'If I do this, will you buy?'

One of the key drivers behind the success of Weight Watchers and similar groups is that the members give a public commitment to each other. This makes the commitment very difficult to go back on without losing face.

So, if you are closing a sale and the client asks for a discount, then you might say, 'If I can get you x off the price, then you will buy it, won't you? In this way, you get their commitment to buy it before you confirm the discount. One of my clients in York is now using this to very powerful effect, when a big supplier asks for a discount. (See also Chapter 15 Know how to bargain.)

Interestingly, when a client fills in their own order form, they are less likely to change their mind and cancel the order.

How language affects you and the other side
The power of the word 'because'

 WARNING!

When you are asking for something in your negotiations, make sure you give a reason – 'the because factor'.

Ellen Langer, a psychologist at the Harvard Business School, did some important research into the use of the word *because* and the effect it had on people.

She performed an experiment* in which students jumped the queue to use a photocopier, using three different approaches:

1. 'Excuse me. I have five pages. May I use the photocopier?' 60 per cent allowed queue jumping.

2. 'Excuse me, I have five pages. May I use the photocopier *because* I'm in a rush?' 94 per cent allowed queue jumping.

3. 'Excuse me, I have five pages. May I use the photocopier *because* I have to make some copies?' 93 per cent allowed queue jumping, even when the excuse was completely ridiculous.

The experiment was linked to mindlessness and how people do not concentrate/listen to many things that are going on during the day, due to repetition and the monotony of the situation they find themselves in. It was the presence of the word *because* that made it easier to jump the queue.

*Source: Langer, E., Blank, A., and Chanowitz, B. (1978). The mindlessness of ostensibly thoughtful action: The role of 'placebic' information in interpersonal interaction. *Journal of Personality and Social Psychology*, 36, 635–642.

TIP TOP TIP!
You will have noticed that a number of these principles overlap. Of course they do, that is why you should use as many as possible, linked together with genuine authenticity.

The Starbucks negotiator meets many of the secrets of influence

I like meeting people for refreshments in a nice coffee store to discuss deals.

1. It is neutral ground.
2. The tables are round.
3. I insist on buying the coffee.
4. It does not take up much time. It is informal.
5. People generally feel comfortable.

Important note on influencing and bargaining

At this point I need to make a comment about the difference between influencing and bargaining. Here, in the influencing chapter, we talk about the power of giving something for nothing (reciprocity). Giving unconditionally to build rapport and psychologically to sow the seeds that the other person owes you something in return.

In Chapter 15 Know how to bargain, we talk about never giving things for nothing, trading everything.

Bargaining is normally where we are actually closing the negotiation, coming to a conclusion, as opposed to influencing the other person. The key words in bargaining are, 'If you do this for us, then we will do that for you.' Making the concession conditional.

However, you might give something small away at the beginning of the bargaining session, as a gesture, to see what happens next.

> 'Words hold power and influence. So choose your words carefully.'

Words influence, they create energy and they create action. The words that you choose are key.

Whether you are using words to yourself, internal dialogue, or to others, words either empower you to move forward or take you backwards. Words are energising or energy sapping.

Generally, people like people who are positive in a business situation. Here are just some words that are power enhancing, positive and energising. Each one starts with a different letter of the alphabet. What are yours?

The A–Z of amazing words

Amazing	Neutron
Brilliant	Outstanding
Curious	Powerful
Delightful	Quantum
Extraordinary	Rich
Fantastic	Sensational
Great	Tremendous
Huge	Unbelievable
Incredible/inspirational	Vivacious
Jubilant	Wonderful
Knock-out	Xtraordinary
Lovely	Yes Yes Yes
Magnificent	Zen

Words that sell

These are some of the words that can help you to sell, from Ted Nicholas – the researcher on language.

Remember, you have to be congruent and have a product or service that helps the customer.

New methods of . . .	This is the solution
Secrets of . . .	Most important
Now is the time . . .	Free
Amazing	How much is this idea worth?
Facts you . . .	You will love the way . . .
At last	Bargain
Assuming	Yes
Breakthrough	Bargain
Here is a way to . . .	YES
The real truth of . . .	The steps towards . . .

Sensory clues to influence

Everyone has a preferred channel for communicating. Some are visual, approximately 60 per cent of people. Some are auditory, approximately 20 per cent of people. Others are kinaesthetic, again 20 per cent of people.

Which of these are your preferred channels? And, more importantly, listen to your clients, the people you are negotiating with and pick up their channel. The more you connect with people, the more they will like you. The more they like you, the more you will be able to persuade, influence and negotiate successfully with them.

Here are examples of the three channels:

- I see what you mean (visual).
- I hear what you are saying (auditory).
- I understand what you are getting at (kinaesthetic).
- Someone's appearance is key to me (visual).
- The sound of someone's voice tells me a lot about them (auditory).

- I can tell more about someone from their handshake (kinaesthetic).

The best marketers/sales people use all three types in their general presentations, communications and negotiations. For example, in a negotiation:

- Can you *see* how that would work, if we agree that?
- How does that *sound* to you as part of the contract?
- Does that option in the negotiation *make sense* to you?

Recap

- Familiarise yourself with the strategies.
- Put as many strategies in place before you negotiate the deal.
- Remember, people will spend more time with you and answer your questions more accurately if they perceive you are like them.
- Choose your language/words carefully.
- And, finally – your clients will enjoy negotiating with you, as these strategies, if done with integrity, are basic to human nature.

15.
Know how to bargain

In this chapter you will learn:

- The importance of understanding the psychology of bargaining.
- Some critical bargaining skills.
- Day-to-day handy haggling hints.
- Ideas that work well in the bargaining and haggling process of the negotiation.

Introduction

Bargaining or haggling starts when you are at the negotiating table, or on the phone, and you start moving closer to where the other side is. The words have similar meanings in English.

We will never know exactly the zone of potential agreement but we will have made our own calculations and have made assessments of the other side's, taking into account all the known and unknown factors.

So, it is time to move. Who makes the first move? There are a lot of opinions on this. Some say you should make the first concession; others say you should let the other side make it. There are people who even say the person who makes the first concession loses.

I do not agree with any of them. The answer is it depends on the circumstances.

However, there can be a case to make a small concession to get the ball rolling, to see if they reciprocate. What they do will give you a valuable insight to their strategy. However, remember the phrase 'Concessions are not contagious.' They may not reciprocate, so you might want to make your move conditional on getting something back in return. That is where the phrase *conditional bargaining* comes from.

Definitions – is there a difference between bargaining and haggling?

These are my definitions of bargaining and haggling. You will see different definitions in different books. However, they amount to same thing.

The process of getting closer to a win win win position, by bargaining or haggling our way to a negotiated agreement.

> *Bargaining* – for a longer-term relationship. Negotiating an annual contract with a supplier. Renegotiating an existing deal. Looking at a longer-term contract.
>
> *Haggling* – more likely to be for a one-off transaction. In the marketplace, in a shop for a one-off purchase.

On a recent seminar, there was a lady from Holland, who did not understand the word haggling. It would appear there are different words in different languages that might not translate exactly to the bargaining and haggling process. In the USA it is called dickering.

Bargaining and haggling is an attitude, make it fun

Your attitude at the start of the negotiation will have a major impact on the results you achieve. People like to deal with others who have a positive attitude to life and to business. You will make it easier for everyone to talk and concede in an atmosphere of positivity.

Make haggling fun. Particularly in a retail, business or market environment, negotiation should be fun. Negotiate with a smile on your face and make ridiculously low offers as your first proposition.

Haggling is expected in some countries, particularly the further south you go in Europe and in many Asian countries.

Take the circumstances and the culture into account. Google the culture to see what comes up.

Get in the right state

A few basics before you start:

1. *Get your brain right, psyche up* – get in the right state/frame of mind before you negotiate. Take a little time on your own and

get your thought process running in the appropriate mode. A series of spoken 'yes's' will get you into 'yes' mode for anything that happens.

2. *Use positive language* – it is easier for people to understand what you are saying if you phrase your words in positive language. Avoid the use of linguistic negatives, such as – do not, cannot, etc.

3. *Reframe unhelpful comments* – when the other party makes a negative statement – reframe it by asking, 'Do you mean . . . and phrasing it in positive language. 'After all, every problem is an opportunity, one man's meat is another man's poison and the glass can be either half full or half empty!'

4. *Make certain your 'self-talk' is positive* – ensure that the words you say inside your mind are focusing on positive outcomes and a positive process. Eradicate any negative doubts and thoughts, as they will damage your external language patterns and, subsequently, damage your results.

Bargaining

Bargaining and haggling are totally interlinked and cannot be too compartmentalised. I prefer to make a slight differentiation for clarity of where they might be more likely to be used, so this section will focus on bargaining.

However, try the techniques in both areas and see how your general negotiating improves and your income/profits increase.

'The more I practise, the luckier I get.'
GARY PLAYER

Give yourself room to manoeuvre

When you are negotiating, you can always come down in price. Come down in the concessions you make. When I say concessions, I mean the totality of the value by which you come down and the totality of the value by which they increase.

I mentioned variables in Chapter 6 Prepare and plan. Variables are the extras, over and above price, which increase or decrease the value to the other side.

So, by starting with a higher offer, your best position, you can come down. If this is not accepted, then you can ask good questions and consider the reason why it is not accepted.

However, the start price should be high *but* realistic and not so high that it loses credibility. This is a judgement you have to make, depending on the circumstances.

> *You can always reduce your price.*

It is a bit like skiing: you can always go down but, to go up, it is a long climb back up, if you have started too low down.

What I mean here is that it is easy to find a reason to bring your price down – checking the figures, reworking the spreadsheets, the fixed, the variable, the marginal costs that are attributed to the product. Spend time working on these with your people.

However, it is not easy from the client's point of view to persuade them to accept an increase in a price suggested yesterday that they have already firmly got in their mind.

Anchor the price

Anchoring the price is a tactic in bargaining that puts the suggestion in the other side's mind that the price and the value are high. They will have to work very hard to get the price to come down and, if they are successful, they will have got a fantastic deal.

For example – 'Our normal price for this product is £10,000. However, in certain circumstances, for a longer-term deal for favourable payment terms, we may be able move it down quite substantially.'

So, rather than starting at a lower price, the seller is anchoring a higher price, the £10,000, and therefore anchoring the perceived value to the other side and others.

Conversely, in order to anchor a lower price, the buyer might say, 'We pay only around £3,000 for this type of product, so you had better sharpen your price.' Even if they are expecting to pay much more than that, they are anchoring a lower price in the mind of the seller.

When the movement does come, it feels to the other side that they have got a big concession and, therefore, psychologically, a great deal.

This is a key tactic in union negotiations, to anchor a high request to see what happens.

Never accept the first offer

Accepting the first offer is a sign of a poor negotiator. The feeling it creates either at the time or later – when the negotiator has slept on it – is that they can go back and get some more concessions or even abort/sabotage the deal. If you accept the first offer the other side makes, the problem is that they will leave feeling that they should have asked a higher price.

If I put my regional franchise business on sale for a fee of £75,000 and someone comes along and offers me £75,000, how do I feel?

I feel that, perhaps, I could have got more for it; I wonder if I have been badly advised; I wonder if they know something I do not know.

So, if you come along and offer me £65,000 for the business, we haggle and then agree a figure of £71,250, do I feel better after the haggled deal or after the higher deal? Psychologically, in your mind, it is the lower one.

DO NOT ACCEPT THE FIRST OFFER

A client of mine bought a property in Sandbanks, Dorset. She made an offer £10,000 under the asking price and the offer was accepted immediately. She spent the next two months worrying that there was something wrong with the property. If the seller had haggled, she would not have worried so much!

Trade concessions

Trade everything. Make all concessions that you give conditional on getting something in return, preferably of a higher value.

Make them conditional: use conditional language such as, 'If you can do X for us, then we would be able to do Y for you.'

The language you might use depends on the circumstances. Generally, it is better to use *third party conditional language*: 'If you can do this for us, then we can do this for you.' Or, although this is more aggressive and a little less win win, you could say, *'We might be able to do this for you.'*

If you have a personal relationship and you are trying to make the negotiations friendlier, you might use, 'If you can do this for me, then I can do this for you.'

> **T!P TOP TIP!**
> Concessions are not contagious. People will not always return the concession. Make sure you get something in return.

It is better to ask for what you want, before you mention what you can do, what you are trading. People tend to hear what is mentioned first. So, if they hear you mention what you are going to concede first, they may switch off to what you want in return.

The key words are, *'If you . . . then we . . .'*

Do not give things for nothing

If someone asks you for something, even if, as far as you are concerned, it is not worth anything to you, the fact they have asked for it means it has a value to them.

Suddenly, it might become a variable that you have not thought of (see Chapter 6 Prepare and plan for more on variables).

So, put it to one side, park it until you have got all their demands and what you are going to ask for clear, and then trade the concessions.

Think about the value of what they are asking for and see how you can trade it in the haggling process.

It could be good to list them on a piece of paper or on a flip chart. You might be able to devalue what you are asking for and increase the perceived value of what they are asking for. That should be your goal.

Be careful of saying 'No problem'

This probably means that they have just asked you for something and you have given them something that they wanted for nothing, that is, without trading it for something in return.

When you are asked, take a quick time out and consider all the things that they might want and you might want before you trade.

 WARNING!

If you are about to say, 'No problem', stop yourself. You might be giving something away that, otherwise, you might trade.

Make the other side feel that they have won something of great value whenever you give a concession. Increase in their mind the relative value.

Separate the people from the problem

Very often negotiations can get personal and, therefore, emotional. Once emotion creeps in, the logical thinking process for a win win deal tends to go out of the window.

This is not helpful for the achievement of goals and people then start thinking about what they are going to get, compared with what you are going to get.

The issue with this is that value is a perception and it is hard to value anything. Value is only what someone will pay for it at a given time.

I have been involved in negotiations where the issue is valuing shares in private companies. The valuation will always be subjective and, no matter what expert professional valuers you bring in, they will have different opinions. There are always different processes of valuing the business or the assets.

A business could be valued on an annual multiple of profits, on a turnover basis or what similar businesses have changed hands for recently.

So, if there are different interpretations of value, then the goal has to be to maximise the value for both parties and work together to that goal, rather than argue amongst each other, let personal prejudices creep in and even jealousy.

Often in partnership breakups, this is what happens. People have got on for a number of years building a successful business. Then, one of the party's life situation changes or one person has different ambitions from the other person and they fall out.

The most difficult issues can happen when marriages break up. I heard a story once where the main assets of the marriage were shares in a private company. So, the valuation was a huge negotiation and a judgement. When they finally came to a settlement, the legal bill amounted to £520,000 on assets of £1.4 million. Getting hung up on what each other has done, and who is going to get what, rather than concentrating on the problem and trying to solve it. Hardly a win win win.

Funny money – price transactions in odd amounts

Funny money is where a contract is priced, or the price is reduced to a number that looks like it has been calculated carefully. For example, 'We can produce this for £9,643.00.' It may have been calculated carefully or it may have been a judgement. However, it might look more realistic than £9,500.00 to the other side, even though it is above the £9,500 you would have gone down to.

When figures are precise, they have verisimilitude and, psychologically, are regarded as more considered and more calculated.

It can be quite useful when you reduce your price. By reducing it to an odd amount, it does not look like you have just come down 10 per cent. If you come down to a round amount, to the other side it may look like you have further to go, whereas an odd amount looks like it has been calculated carefully.

Flinching on the price

Flinching is jargon in negotiating for acting surprised when the other side makes an offer. It comes in all formats. From the gentle, 'You are joking,' to the more aggressive outrage that some people seem to enjoy.

When someone says, 'It costs X,' you simply might squint and draw breath before asking, 'How much?' in an enquiring, surprised tone of voice. It also might come with a scratch of the head, emphasising the visual surprise as well as the verbal surprise.

Use silence to good effect – listen more than talk

Control your emotions. If someone has made an unreasonable demand, do not rise to the bait, but remain silent for a few seconds. This should cause the other party to reconsider or justify the demand. Make notes, if necessary.

Ask –

How can we get a deal? If you do not ask, you do not get. And, if you do not ask, you do not give the other side the opportunity to say yes.

> **T!P TOP TIP!**
> Say, 'We are working together – we do want a deal, don't we?'

Go for a win win win scenario

Try to reach an amicable, wise and equitable conclusion so that both sides come away with the feeling that they got a good deal. Seek to strengthen long-term relationships through the negotiation process.

Feelings often are of more value than a deal where you have squeezed the other side past the point where they are a little unhappy.

Summarising

During the bargaining process in a complicated negotiation, make sure both parties understand what has been agreed.

Make notes of concessions gained and granted as you go along. Stop for periodic summaries of the position. This avoids any misunderstanding and prevents people going back on what they have already agreed.

Often, I might use a flip chart or a big piece of paper in a big meeting so people can see what has been agreed. One of the reasons for this is that people who are not listening can see what is written up. Unless they disagree immediately, you have got agreement by default.

I would always put a flip chart in a negotiating room, just in case you need to use it on the spur of the moment. This is all part of the preparation.

If you have no flip charts, then use an A3 or A4 pad and put it in the middle of the desk so everybody can see it all the time.

If this does not happen, then ensure you make your own clear notes, in case the other side comes back and disagrees and you cannot remember. Clarity is important.

I was in a negotiation, acting for a client, and the other side did not seem to have the integrity that I expected. At the end of the meeting, we both said we would write the contract. They insisted and I smelt a rat. In our debrief, we wrote down exactly our perception of what had been agreed. When the contract came in 10 days later, they had, materially, altered one of the clauses outside our agreement. We called them and reopened the negotiation of the clauses.

Do not be the first to make a major concession

Do not be the first to make a major concession. This makes you appear too eager and weakens your position. Minor concessions to get the ball rolling are quite in order.

Concession making is an interesting game in psychology. Watch how they tend to do it and see what normally happens from your previous company encounters.

Some people advise, make the concessions small and then smaller. It depends on where you have started and the circumstances of the negotiation.

Avoid 'splitting the difference'

Avoid splitting the difference, unless that puts you in an advantageous position. The person who offers to split the difference is conceding half of what they asked for originally, without trading any concession. It is acceptable to split the difference for small amounts or when there is very little at stake.

This suggestion often leads to an inequitable result, especially where it is made when the time for negotiation is running out. Some people would take the suggestion as a 50 per cent concession and negotiate on the other 50 per cent.

I remember doing this after I came back from studying at the Harvard Negotiation Programme in the Boston masterclass. A client rang me up and said, 'Let's split the difference.' I replied, 'I cannot split 50/50, but I could go 70/30.' She agreed immediately.

Leave some meat on the bone

Always ensure that the other party makes a profit and feels good about the transaction you have struck. If you take all the profit away, you will damage the long-term relationship and may receive both second-rate goods and services.

Always ask twice

When haggling, having received the first discounted offer, always ask for a second bite of the cherry – particularly if their first offer is stated as a round figure, such as 10 per cent or 5 per cent. Then you know there is more to be had. Say, 'Surely you can do a little better than that? How much can I have this for?' You will make them feel better and get a better price for yourself. Do not forget to smile when you are saying it.

Watch out for the nibble

Just when you think you have got agreement, the other side comes back and asks for another concession. You may have agreed the price and they then ask for another discount. You may have agreed the delivery date and then they ask for it earlier. You may have agreed the payment terms and then they ask for the money earlier.

Children are fantastic at using this tactic, asking for one thing and, when it is agreed, asking for something else.

Make sure you have everything on the table before you start agreeing to requests.

If they still want something else, then ask for something back in return. For example, 'If we give you this . . . we need . . . from you.'

Soften the blow

When you have to give people bad news – such as a price rise, or you cannot meet the person's price – do this over a longer period, lowering expectations and then offer a slightly better price than expected.

Use 'What if ...' statements

Do this to fact find. This way you will understand what might be acceptable to the other side. However, make sure that they fully understand that you are not making an offer, but simply exploring possibilities: 'What if we do this . . .', 'What if we do . . .'

Set aside issues that cannot be resolved instantly

If you cannot resolve an issue, move on to one that can be agreed immediately. Take the difficult issues to one side and 'park them', coming back to them later. This has the effect of being able to agree most of the points and helps the other party come towards an agreement on the outstanding points. They will have invested a great deal of time in 80 per cent of the items, which were easy to agree, why jeopardise the deal now?

Involve advisers and coaches (get a second opinion)

The time spent trying to see how the price can be increased for everyone is time well spent.

Coming up with alternatives can be productive for you and your organisation – seek solutions that create agreement rather than conflict.

I work with clients to see how we can maximise their position and leave a win win win relationship intact.

Have price lists

People tend to believe things that are written down. In the mind of the other person, they give authority that the price is right. Price lists are very effective for that. They tend to stop many people even thinking of haggling. Do not be put off yourself. Think of it as just a tactic to stop you haggling.

TIP TOP TIP!

How you concede is more important than *what* you concede for preserving long-term relationships. Make the other side feel good.

Variables

Do not forget to have a list of your variables when you come to trade concessions, together with a list of what variables you think they might be able to give you. (See more on variables in Chapter 6 Prepare and plan.)

People issues – when you are bargaining and haggling

It is so easy to get charged up emotionally about any situation. Here are a few people issues that will help you to let go emotionally.

Separate the people from the problem

Whilst you are feeling emotional about the buying and selling process, you will not negotiate your best deal. Let go! Realise that there are always other suppliers and always other buyers in the market. Seldom will you have only one choice.

When you decide emotionally that you want something, like a car, a house or a big item, you reduce your bargaining position. The fact that you want it, rather than have any other option, will send a signal to the other side, unless you are a very good poker player (and haggling is, generally, like poker).

> 'Travel a mile in the other person's moccasins.'
> ANON

There are two sides to everything – no matter how thin you slice it

Look at the situation from their point of view – understand what their objectives are and where they might be coming from.

Ask yourself a question

Ask yourself, 'If I were them, what would be the 10 key issues for me?' Put this question at the top of a plain piece of paper and write down the answers as quickly as you can, without pausing. Show it to other people involved and ask them to add their thoughts.

Ask others

How would others see it from their perspective? Remember, there are nearly seven billion people in the world and everyone has a different thumb print, eye retina print and, therefore, perhaps a different perception of what you are haggling about.

Remember the two young girls arguing over an orange

When two young girls were arguing over an orange, finally they asked each other why they wanted it. One said, 'I want the peel to make marmalade.' The other admitted she wanted to squeeze it to make orange juice. Find out what the other person wants. It may well be that you both can have what you want.

Anticipate all their moves

You should not negotiate/haggle until you can be certain that you have considered every move the other party is likely to make. Make sure you have checked thoroughly with everyone on your team.

Realise it is the process not the price

Blunt price negotiation is difficult for everyone concerned. Conversation over a few minutes, building a relationship and rapport ensures that everyone walks away smiling.

The price is only one factor. People always buy people before they buy the item or its price.

> **T!P TOP TIP!**
> Good negotiators have double vision. They can see things from both sides. Put yourself in the other person's shoes.

Haggling – tips for buying

'The well-skilled haggler has an 80 per cent chance of bagging a bargain.'
RESHMA RUMSEY, TV REPORTER, *ITV'S SURVIVAL STREET*

In the first part of this chapter, I talked about bargaining; now let us have a look at haggling. If you do not intend to have a long-term relationship with the other side, then probably you will be haggling.

Many people do not like haggling but, if you do not haggle, then you are going to be paying more than perhaps you need to, most of the time.

It is seldom that we get a discount if we go into a buying situation not expecting to get one. Be positive and you will be amazed how easy it is when you ask the right questions. Look for what you might be able to do for the other person in return.

Whilst people think that many of these situations are only for the marketplace, often we are operating in a business marketplace where these concepts should be used.

If you do not haggle, then other people will get the rewards of extra profit that you deserve.

Practising haggling in shops and marketplaces will help immensely in business.

THE SIMPLE PROCESS

Here is a simple process that you can follow for any haggling situation:

1. Find the decision maker.
2. Build rapport.
3. Make them an offer.
4. If they make a counter offer, make them one or change the parameters to variables.
5. Close the deal, if you want it.

TIP TOP TIP!

Learn when the numbers are small. Take every opportunity to practise your haggling skills when numbers are small.

Having fun and buying a second-hand item in a car boot sale far below the asking price, will be the same mindset and methods used in many of your major negotiations through life. A few pounds saved at the market stall may teach you to save thousands at the board table.

Haggling ideas related to prices and discounts
NEVER PAY RETAIL

A good question to use whilst haggling is, 'I never pay the recommended retail price or the asking price. Is that OK?'

Provided that you say this with a smile on your face and in a good humour, many people will respond with a simple, 'Yes.'

Now you can have an easy conversation to provide a win win win arrangement.

USE THE AUTHORITY QUESTION
When buying in a wholesale/retail outlet, ask the counter assistant,

'Do you have the authority to give discounts?'

> *If the answer is, 'Yes'*, you will know that discounts are available. Simply ask, 'How much can you do this for?'

> *If the answer is 'No'*, ask 'Who does?'

USE THE CREDIT CARD METHOD
When you know you have reached a point of agreement on price, offer credit card payment or a slightly better price for cash. Many outlets have to pay the credit card company a percentage of sales when credit cards are used. The retailer often will prefer to give you that percentage for a cash deal.

CHECK THE PAPER WORK
Where companies use an order form, you will find that often there is a designated space for discount. They even put it on the form! If you see that word, make certain to ask, 'How much discount is available?'

MATCH THE PRICE
Make sure you do your research as to the other prices that are available in the marketplace. Many companies will match other suppliers' prices. You have to ask simply: 'Will you match your competitor's prices?' Then buy from the most reliable supplier.

'Will you price match?' – remember that the cheapest price might not have the best service, if you think you might need help/follow up/spares, etc.

ASK FOR GOODS NOT DISCOUNT

If a discount is not available, then ask for goods instead. Very often a supplier will be happy to add a bonus item rather than lower their price.

ASK FOR THE MULTIPLE PRICE

In order to find out the lowest price possible, ask for the price for a number of items.

This will give you an indication as to how low the price could be. Then you may well be able to negotiate that low price for just one item.

Haggling – tips for selling and closing the deal

Always ask for the order

When you are the seller in a negotiation, do not leave without asking for the order. You have put in the hard work and now is the time to reap your just rewards. A simple, 'Shall we go ahead, then?' may be all you need. Whichever words you use to ask that closing question, make certain you do!

Suggest an alternative

One of the oldest and most honest ways to close a transaction is to suggest an alternative: 'Would you like the red one or the blue one?' This assumes the conclusion of the deal and offers a simple alternative.

Similarly, there is the double bind – 2 options close

A double bind, as it is called in psychology, is where you give the other side two options. However, they are minor points.

'Would you like it in white or red?'

'Would you like it delivered on a Tuesday or a Thursday?'

> A client of mine used it on her husband, a couple of days after a course. He wanted her to get the bus to the shops. She asked him, 'Would you like me to use the car or will you drop me off in town?'

Close on a minor point

If someone agrees to a minor point of the transaction, they are, in effect, agreeing to the whole transaction. For example: 'Do you want a balcony and sea view?' If this question is answered with a yes, then the person is highly unlikely to refuse to book the holiday.

Close early in the conversation

It is never too soon to test close, to find out the real intent of the other party. Ideal test closes use questions such as:

'Does this make sense so far?'

'Is this OK with you?'

'Does this sound good?'

'Does this look right?'

Any excess conversation, after agreement has been reached, may make the other party reconsider their options and your position.

Do not celebrate too enthusiastically. If you are too enthusiastic, the other side will believe that they struck the wrong deal. Be happy but not too happy!

Calculate the real cost of concessions

When giving concessions, make sure you always calculate them, based on the profit line, not the turnover line.

For example, if a company usually makes a net profit of, say, 10 per cent, and a negotiator gives away 5 per cent on a sale, the 5 per cent represents 50 per cent of profit!

Use soft pound deals or bartering

There are times when an exchange of goods or expertise might be better than an exchange of money. Generally, this applies to short-term transactions. I gave my local golf club some marketing ideas for how to do a newsletter, in exchange for a year's membership.

Handle threats

Handle threats in an uncompromising way.

Recognise a threat as something to weaken your position and your resolve. Hold the silence. When they have made a threat, people expect you to react and the mere fact that you do not do so often means they qualify what they have said.

Many people find this silence very uncomfortable. If you find it uncomfortable, make some notes on your pad and then look up and say something like, 'That is interesting. Why did you say that?' If necessary, take a break, time out or an adjournment, as these have the same effect of cooling things down and give you some thinking time.

This also gives some quality time with your own team to discuss rationally the issues.

Leave when the deal is done

Once the agreement has been reached, do not spend too much time socialising. Sign the papers, thank the other party for their agreement, shake hands and go!

Agreements and contracts

Parity contracts

A parity contract is one where it says in the detail that you will receive no less than any other client. It is prevalent in some sports contracts when there is a superstar who can call the shots. If the team buys someone else, then the superstar's income matches the new person, if it is more.

If someone wants me to speak for a lower fee than normal, and they have a good reason, then I might agree, 'I will do it, as long as you can confirm you have not paid anybody any more than this in the past.'

Service contracts

Agree the fee and contract before the service is delivered.

Agree the amount of the payment or the concessions up front, as their value will diminish as time passes when the service has been given. This is similar to the plumber who spends five minutes at your house fixing a leak and then tries to charge you a small fortune. He needs agreement of the price up front while the water is pouring through the ceiling.

Do not forget

You must always have a walk away position. Sometimes, just walk away – walk out and see what happens. You can always change your mind and go back.

If you do not have a walk away position, you may leak this information to the other side in your body language.

Note that in trained negotiation situations, for example buying a car, generally the salesperson will not take you seriously, unless you get to the door and are walking out.

Some language that will help you when bargaining and haggling

- 'That is outside my budget! What can you do to help us?'
- 'If I pay that my partner/wife will go crazy.'
- 'My boss expects me to get a discount. Could you help me?'
- 'My chairman Derek will give me a really hard time/go crazy if I pay that.'
- 'I have to justify this to my board. They will shoot me if I agree.' (Said whilst smiling, of course.)
- 'I am being coached by Derek Arden. How will I justify it to him that I paid the full price?'
- 'I am in a competition to see who can get the best discounts.'
- 'Is there any flexibility on price?' (Closed question.)
- 'I need some flexibility on price.'
- 'Is there something you can do to help me on price?'
- 'Could you sharpen your pencil?'
- 'And the usual discount, please.'
- 'That price does not work for me. Can you do something to help me?'

Recap

- The magic words for trading concessions are 'If you do . . . for us, then we would be able to do . . . for you.'

- You can always start high and come down, whereas it is very difficult to start low and go up.

- List your variables and value to the other side.

- Remember be bold. Haggling is not relationship negotiating. Always ask and ask again. Push the envelope with a smile on your face.

- Do not get emotional about what you are buying. Buy if the price is right. Do not buy it, if you do not want it, just because the price is good.

16.
Know how to handle conflict

In this chapter you will learn:

- Inevitably, there will be elements of conflict in negotiations.

- There are five different conflict styles, according to the researchers.

- How to adapt your conflict style.

- How to understand your style and the style of others.

Introduction

T!P TOP TIP!
Some degree of conflict is almost always present in a negotiation situation.

In any negotiation situation you will encounter conflict in differing degrees. You need to understand the best and most effective way of handling it, taking into account your personality and style.

Many people view conflict like they view a row, a disagreement, a rant or how they feel when they are almost coming to blows.

Conflict is much wider than that and we have many different types of conflict every day, often requiring the use of negotiating to resolve it.

It is another one of those issues in life where you have to learn to deal with it in a win win way to make your life more pleasant and more tenable.

Definition of conflict:

'Any situation where your concerns or desires differ from another person.'

It is human nature not to enjoy conflict. To avoid conflict is an intuitive thing in most people, as conflict has consequences!

However, remember that there have been only 26 days since 1945 when there has not been a war going on anywhere around the world. In these circumstances, we need to accept that there will be conflict and deal with it in a sensible and professional way.

Business conflict

Business conflict arises many times a day, when people are chasing and negotiating their own goals, own agendas and trying to achieve the highest price and the lowest costs.

I often ask people, on a scale of 0–100, how big is this conflict situation? I then explain that 1 is a minor disagreement, such as what to have for dinner with your partner, and 100 is a conflict like a world war. Then I might ask what you think you have to do to sort it out. This tends to focus their minds on how important it is and what the consequences might be.

The scoring tends to get things into perspective, particularly when emotions are running high.

T!P TOP TIP!

Sometimes, as negotiators, we have to create a little conflict to get the best price for our products and pay the lowest price for our purchases.

When you set a goal to get a better deal, you will always have a degree of conflict with the other side. Even when your aim is a win win outcome.

Is conflict healthy?

Some people may see conflict as just healthy competition whereas others might see it as pressure and stress deliberately played to provoke a reaction.

Personalities and behaviours

The rational person

The rational person likes to look logically at all the data, the information, the personalities and how they are reacting before making a negotiating decision. They would want an intellectual discussion before action is taken. They are uncomfortable negotiating, without first finding out all the facts. They will not like the conflict that it creates but must learn to deal with it, to achieve the rational outcome.

The sensitive person

The sensitive person wants to make sure that everyone is in agreement and wants to help them solve their problems and issues. If there is disagreement, often they will take the comments personally. More than anyone, they have to make sure the negotiation is separated from the personalities, to handle the conflict in their own mind.

> **T!P TOP TIP!**
> Separate the people from the problem.

The ambitious person

The ambitious person wants it to be their way or the highway. They are driven towards achieving their goals. 'Why isn't it done yet?' is what you will hear from them. Often, they are surrounded by people who will not argue, who are used to their behaviour.

They do not like the behaviour of the rational person, as they see them as someone who is slowing them down or stopping them from achieving their targets and goals. They have little time for the sensitive person's feelings. They tend to get their way by creating conflict.

Conflict can be good in a creative stimulating situation!

A friend of mine creates conflict to stimulate discussion when we are brainstorming issues in the strategy meetings of the Professional Speaking Association. I know him well and know what he is doing.

But, sometimes, the people who do not understand this can take offence, as he does it quite aggressively. If we do this, we need to do it sensitively, taking in the different personalities and styles, in order to be more effective. If we do not, residual ill feeling can be left.

> **T!P TOP TIP!**
> Without challenge you don't stimulate new ideas and change which is necessary in today's unbelievably fast world.

Resilience is important

You can learn how to be more resilient in a negotiation by understanding what is going on better.

> **T!P TOP TIP!**
> Resilient people manage conflict better.

I have had to learn to be more resilient, as I have progressed to be a better negotiator.

Resilient people are able to take the disagreement as part of the problem-solving debate, rather than take it personally, unless the comments are personal, which needs different handling. They stay open minded and have learnt to use their inter-personal skills to handle the disagreement.

As a negotiator, you have to get used to conflict and use it to your advantage, even if, probably, you do not like it.

> **T!P TOP TIP!**
> When you recognise conflict occurring, stop. Take a breath, a mini time out, and accept it as part of the negotiating process.

Understanding your conflict style is very useful!

As we have discussed, conflict is a fact of life.

In negotiations, often you will have conflict, whether it is in business, your career or life, and disputes will arise with clients and customers and, internally, with partners and friends.

Also, you will react differently under different conditions and with different people. Remember that people tend to act marginally differently, in different circumstances.

Conflict can be damaging, if not handled well, so your negotiation style is a critical variable when negotiating.

It is very useful to understand your style in order to be self-aware and adjust your style whenever you recognise that it might be beneficial.

The Thomas-Kilmann Conflict Mode Instrument

Kenneth W. Thomas and Ralph H. Kilmann are experts who have studied conflict over many years.

They have developed a questionnaire called the Thomas-Kilmann Conflict Mode Instrument (TKI). This is one of the most popular psychological profiling instruments available.

TKI is used in negotiating training, crisis intervention, marriage and family counselling and for improving performance when coaching and mentoring.

TKI is available from OPP, Oxford, England OX2 8EP or from www. opp.com.

Never forget that you have choices in conflict. All five conflict handling styles are available to you. This knowledge gives you a greater sense of control, enabling you to steer conflicts in different directions by using a different style.

I have used it in coaching and negotiation masterclasses for many years, with many people, varying from healthcare workers, to personal assistants, to finance directors, sales executives and to directors of large corporations and charities.

The results are very useful to the person, by looking at, analysing and reflecting on their own personalities.

It is also very useful to consider the styles of others and how you can recognise other patterns of behaviour.

This is my take on the instrument and what you can learn from it to make you a better negotiator.

The TKI instrument recognises five conflict styles (behaviours when faced with conflict) and one or two of these, generally, will be your natural default style(s). In other words, the style you prefer when under pressure and you have not had time to think about changing your natural behaviour.

Like all of these types of questionnaires, they are general, but I have found this remarkably accurate and effective when working closely with more than a thousand people.

The styles are listed below. However, one of the questions that often I am asked is:

How might I find out the style of someone I meet for the first time?

1. *Observing their initial behaviour is quite useful.* The way they greet you, the way they build rapport or not, one or two things they do or say. You need to switch your sensory awareness on and be alert to this in those first few minutes.

2. *Handshakes.* Interestingly, there seems to be a correlation in the way people shake hands. An aggressive hand on top with a hard squeeze tends to indicate a competitive person. An upright shake with equal grip seems to indicate a collaborator. If the shake is softer, then the person might be an accommodator. Avoiders often are not that keen to shake hands and often will not make as much eye contact.

The five conflict styles

1. Competing

Competitors are highly assertive and uncooperative. The individual pursues their own issues, goals and concerns at the other person's expense. Many MBA students take this line. They have paid a lot of money to pursue their ambitions and therefore are more likely to be competitive. I try to coach them to make sure they adjust their styles to match the other people, perhaps moving towards a more collaborative style.

This is a power play, a power-orientated mode. Competitors have the ability to argue their own position, their status in life and their rank.

Competing might mean standing up for your rights, defending a position that you believe is correct, or simply trying to win.

Competing people are more likely to take more chances. To them, being strong often means getting more than you. Winning is more important than the relationship and often feelings and concerns are discounted or ignored.

Threats, ultimatums, walking out or threatening to walk out are all part of their normal negotiating tactics. Their mantra is win!

Bullies are competitive.

Sometimes, off-the-scale competitive people are bullies. However, bullies tend not to do much research; they have never had to, as they have used other means of getting their own way. So, being meticulously prepared and anticipating their stance can be a very good way of combating this type of individual.

2. Collaborating (problem solving)

Collaborators are both assertive and cooperative – the opposite of avoiding.

Sometimes this is called problem solving.

Collaborating involves an attempt to work with the other person to find some solution, which fully satisfies the concerns of both persons. Time is required to get together to work out options and attempt to make the 'pie' bigger. Complex diplomatic negotiations often fit into this area. Take the issues in Northern Ireland in the 1990s or in the Middle East now.

If you are determined to work together and have a long-term relationship, then this is the style you want. It is difficult if you are short of time or the other side is intent on playing hardball.

Collaborating means exploring an issue to identify the underlying concerns of the two parties in order to find an alternative that meets both sets of concerns.

Collaborating between two persons might take the form of exploring a disagreement to learn from each other's insights.

3. Compromising

Compromisers are intermediate in both assertiveness and cooperativeness.

The objective should be for an efficient, mutually acceptable solution, which partially satisfies both parties. It falls in a middle ground between competing and accommodating. This conflict style often is used by fair-minded people who want a win win, but you have to be careful, as these people are easier to manipulate by people who just want a win.

Compromising gives up more than competing but less than accommodating.

Likewise, it addresses an issue more directly than avoiding, but does not explore it in as much depth as collaborating.

Compromising might mean splitting the difference, exchanging concessions or seeking a quick middle-ground position.

Generally, compromisers prefer the relationship maintenance rather than being seen to take a personal advantage.

4. Avoiding

Avoiders are unassertive and uncooperative. They do not pursue their own concerns or those of the other person immediately.

They do not address the conflict. Often these people like definitive answers. Avoiders are the types of people who have careers in very structured hierarchies.

Engineers often are avoiders.

Avoiders generally dislike interpersonal conflicts, games with winners and losers and they avoid situations that require open discussions. Peace and quiet is the name of the game in personal and business relationships.

Avoiding might take the form of diplomatically side-stepping an issue, postponing an issue until a better time, or simply withdrawing from a threatening situation.

5. Accommodating

Accommodators are unassertive and cooperative – the opposite of competers.

The personal wants of accommodators satisfy the other person's requests.

When managing accommodators, you have to make sure they do not concede too much. In fact, you have to ensure that you do not give them much room to manoeuvre, as it is likely they will concede as soon as the other person asks, flinches or expresses any disappointment.

Accommodating might take the form of selfless generosity or charity, obeying another person's orders when one would prefer not to, or yielding to another's point of view.

Accommodators do not like the conflict that is created by standing up for your own valid position, trying to obtain any position above the walk away position. If you are managing them, it is best to let them do what they are good at, and do their negotiations for them.

Certainly, don't let them have a wide discretion on what they are allowed to give away in the negotiation. If you do, you know what will happen. They will give the maximum away without getting anything in return.

I have met people who have exceeded their authority in their own company, to satisfy their client's requests. Many of those that I have known end up breaking company rules and getting dismissed.

WARNING
It has been proven that, generally, most people think that their style is the same as the other person's style.

It is useful to imagine a chart or diagram where the vertical axis is the level of assertiveness – and the horizontal axis is the level of cooperativeness.

More assertive styles would be at the top of the left hand axis and less assertive towards the bottom. The further to the right you go, the more cooperative people are. So this means competing styles would be in the top left box with collaborating to the right. Avoiding would be in the bottom left box with accommodating appearing bottom right, leaving compromising in the middle.

The best way to work out your style is to use the TKI assessment. Alternatively and as only a guide, think about the words that fit the five styles and choose the words that you feel most comfortable with. This is more likely to be your preference default style with conflict resolution.

Fill in the TKI conflict mode instrument online or obtain the workbook from Oxford Psychology Press (www.opp.com/tools/).

The instrument can help you minimise conflict and damage to the relationship, helping you to work together. It takes only 10 minutes to complete and I have found the results remarkably accurate. I have used it with thousands of students, delegates and people I have been mentoring.

> **T!P TOP TIP!**
> As a negotiator, we need to understand how to handle conflict, how to use it to our advantage and how we handle ourselves in a conflict situation.

If you just want a guide to your own preference, then look at the words below. See which ones fit your preferred approach to conflict. This is a good quick win.

If you tick more statements in one section, then that is likely to be the style you adopt for conflict resolution.

All five approaches are appropriate at times.

Competing
- [ ] My way or the highway
- [ ] It is really important to win
- [ ] I know I am right
- [ ] I am firm about pursuing my goals
- [ ] I am good at selling the benefits of my position to others

Collaborating
- [ ] Two heads are better than one
- [ ] Let us look at all the issues
- [ ] I like to use a problem-solving approach
- [ ] It is helpful to seek others' views and ideas
- [ ] Let us get all the issues on the table

Compromising
- [ ] Let us strike a deal
- [ ] Shall we split the difference?
- [ ] Let us find the middle ground
- [ ] I will concede on some points if you will
- [ ] It is important to be realistic about this

Avoiding
- [ ] I will think about it tomorrow
- [ ] I hate confrontation

→

- [ ] It is not such a big issue
- [ ] I do not want to make a fuss about this
- [ ] There is no point in bringing this up

Accommodating

- [ ] I would be pleased to help
- [ ] It seems very important to you
- [ ] I often help others get what they want
- [ ] I do not like to hurt people's feelings
- [ ] It is generally more important to preserve the relationship than win the point

All five approaches are correct at the right time. The acid test is understanding when those times are.

T!P TOP TIP!

By understanding that other people have different styles and recognising the style, you can adjust your style to help the situation.

How do you adjust your style?

If you are an accommodator

Typically, you like to give it to people. You grant them what they ask for. You need to adjust your style to stand up to people and negotiate additional fees for extras – or stand your ground. Accommodators like to accommodate.

If you are an avoider

You need to adjust your style so as not to avoid confrontation always. This style is low on assertiveness, so being more assertive in a way that suits your personality will be the first thing to do.

If you are a competitor

You need to learn not to always be competitive. If you are dealing with an accommodator, it is good to back off and reduce your assertiveness and that will help build a better relationship.

If you are a collaborator

You are strong on assertiveness and relationship. Collaborators need to be careful with avoiders and accommodators and to soften a little. However, as with competitors, collaborators need to be careful that the competitor does not take advantage of their relationship style.

The main thing is to be able to adjust your style to meet your objectives. This takes awareness and practice.

If you are a compromiser

Remember that you don't always need to compromise and that won't always get you the best options. You fit nicely in the middle so practise being competitive occasionally and at the other end of the spectrum accommodating.

Here are just some of the things I have coached negotiators on

1. *Simon – a loss adjuster.* Always going for the win, Simon is a *competitor*. He has to be careful of relationships and losing goodwill. He may not know what is going on in his organisation, as people will be scared to tell him any bad news. The problem is that he needs to know that sort of thing early on.

2. *Elizabeth – runs her own business.* Elizabeth is an *accommodator*. She has to be careful because she likes to say yes to everybody. She will not get the best prices for her services. People may take advantage of her accommodating nature and her need to be liked by everyone.

3. *George – a collaborator.* The danger here is you can spend too long trying to get an agreement, which may be inefficient. Competitive people may take advantage of your collaborative nature.

4. *Julie – a compromiser.* The issue is that she might be keen to split the difference and compromise. The other side may not be prepared to do that and so may take advantage of her.

5. *Maureen – an avoider.* Maureen wants to avoid conflict, so she would prefer not to negotiate. If Maureen puts things out for people to bid, she will take the best bid without talking to someone who might expect to negotiate.

Charities

Working with a charity in Oxford, I quickly discovered that they had employed some remarkably hard-working people who did a fantastic job raising donations and helping third-world countries deal with all sorts of issues.

However, I soon discovered that the majority of staff were 'nice people' who avoided conflict and tended to trust people to give them the best price the first time. In reality, this was not what happened. Some suppliers were taking advantage of their good nature.

I coached people to be a bit tougher, to move up the assertive scale when dealing with these issues and to try and get them to understand that it is necessary to be more assertive to achieve the charity's objectives. Generally I have found it is a common trait with people who work in the third sector (the charity and not for profit sector).

 WARNING!

It is estimated that we have conflict 25 per cent of the time in some way or another in business situations.

Mediation

Mediation can be a great way of avoiding conflict going too far. The mediator listens to both sides without forming any judgements. Then they try to find common ground, which avoids the unnecessary expense of lawyers and expensive costs.

Irritators

These are words and phrases that will irritate the other side and cause more conflict.

When I was at the Harvard Business School, they told me that average negotiators would use 10.8 irritators an hour. Yet professional negotiators would use only 2.3 irritators an hour.

Take irritators out of your language.

Here are some examples of irritators:

'It is always the same here.'

' . . . with people like you.'

'You do not understand.'

'Get a grip on your business.'

'Your company is hopeless.'

'You are hopeless.'

'Terrible service.'

'My time is precious.'

'Times have changed for the worse.'

'Why don't you do things properly?'

'Employ more intelligent people instead of donkeys.'

'Read things properly.'

'It is ever since people like you stopped listening.'

'You are always ripping people off.'

'There is no trust these days.'

'The price is ridiculous.'

'There are no extras anymore.'

'Outrageous!'

'Unbelievable!'

'Disgraceful!'

'Insulting!'

'Cannot believe it.'

'You are joking!'

'You are bonkers!'

'It is stupid.'

'I am furious with what has happened.'

Hostility management workshop

I was asked to run a hostility management workshop for a major retailer recently. I was curious about what they expected, as there are no general courses on this subject. I spoke to the team leader and he told me the issues that they have in head office and the hostility they faced.

As I was preparing the material, I thought suddenly to ask him for a typical email exchange. The email exchange showed the persuaders 'barking orders in an aggressive highly threatening tone'. When I suggested that the people they were trying to persuade were, perhaps, pushing back and not putting up with their hostility, the penny dropped.

Gender differences

Male and female research of MBA students at Harvard shows that men are more likely to be competitive and women are more likely to be collaborative.

In addition, it showed that women generally tend to behave more ethically than men and use fewer dirty negotiation tactics.

There have not been many wars started by women.

If you have not got time to fill in the questionnaire, I suggest you take a few minutes to think through your style. Consider the style of others that you know. Try changing your style a little to match theirs and see what happens.

WARNING!
No matter how thin you slice it, there are always two sides to a disagreement.

Recap

- Remember, there are five conflict styles, from competitive to accommodating.
- Learn to adapt your dominant style.

- All styles are good, at the appropriate time.
- If you have a style that is non-assertive, gently raise your assertiveness, as you become a more experienced negotiator.
- If you have a competitive style, learn to read other people and back off, when appropriate.
- Avoid using irritators that will not help the outcome.

17.
Rate your negotiation skills again

	Your skills	Your rating	Multiplier	Your score
1	Prepare and plan	1 2 3 4 5	× 4	....
2	Give a great first impression	1 2 3 4 5	× 1	....
3	Ask the right questions	1 2 3 4 5	× 1	....
4	Listen well	1 2 3 4 5	× 2	....
5	Use your head	1 2 3 4 5	× 1	....
6	Read body language	1 2 3 4 5	× 2	....
7	Watch out for lying	1 2 3 4 5	× 1	....
8	Use the right strategies and tactics	1 2 3 4 5	× 3	....
9	Influence the other side	1 2 3 4 5	× 1	....
10	Know how to bargain	1 2 3 4 5	× 2	....
11	Know how to handle conflict	1 2 3 4 5	× 1	....
12	Confidence when negotiating	1 2 3 4 5	× 1	....
			Total:	....

Re-score yourself now. See how you have improved your scores.

What do you need to work on next?

Re-score yourself in 3 months' time.

Having re-scored yourself, you will have improved in some of the key areas. You will notice that confidence is number 12. This is because the more you discover about numbers 1-11, and the more you practise these skills, the more confident you will become. Confidence comes from information, knowledge, wisdom and practice.

PART 3
HOTSPOTS

Hotspot 1
How to ask for a salary increase

Prove what you are worth

During the year, do a fantastic job. Do more than is required of you. Volunteer for the small things that others shy away from and are easy to do and fix, for example organise the Christmas party or organise the team away day.

Make sure you come across as someone who deserves to be paid more. Be punctual, smart, well dressed and do not be the first to leave the office.

If you work from home, make sure you are emailing the relevant people while you are at home. There seems to be a psychology in many firms that, if you are working from home, probably you are skiving.

Keep the evidence

Keep a record of everything you do during the year or the period on which you are being measured on. Particularly the small things but also bigger things where you contributed to the success of others.

Some people do not give credit to others for the work they did in helping them fulfil a major contract or client relationship. Training people, running courses, speaking at meetings, fixing up a quick presentation after you have been on a course are often the things that do not get noticed or get forgotten about when your appraisal or bonus time comes around.

Write a summary report: a summary of your achievements for the year about three weeks before salary review/appraisal time. Call it something non-threatening when sending it to the recipient, for example 'position report'. You do not want it to look like it is the day before the appraisal and then you are going to ask for a pay rise. However, keep it with you and you can refer to it at the appraisal if it is not mentioned.

This is a softening up tactic and a clear statement of your achievements (see Chapter 13 Use the right strategies and tactics).

Your salary negotiating dossier comes in very useful at this time. A sample is shown in the table below. You could include it, but change the name before you do that, or cut and paste it onto a review of the year sheet.

DATE	PIECE OF WORK	RESULTS	PROFITABILITY
2 July	Organised summer party	Great feedback	Staff morale up
22 July	Presentation to Sainsbury's	Won bid	£10,000

Insist on interim reviews, where you sell what you have been doing to the boss. Some people might call these one to ones. Check how you are doing. Correct anything else they want you to do.

Look at your options

Compare the job market for someone of your skills and find out what similar roles pay. Remember, the type of company depends on what they will pay, so private sector, public sector or not for profit could be vastly different.

The terms and conditions – these are the extras, the potential stress levels, quality of life, commuting, pension fund, days' holiday, health care cover, sickness cover, leniency for days off, childcare, crèches. These are all variables, which I have listed in the following section.

At the appraisal meeting

Make sure you negotiate the highest appraisal, report or summary of the year you can. At least that will give you an idea of how much you may or may not get and your value to the company.

And do not forget the value of company benefits, such as the following:

- job title
- recognition
- flexibility
- accolades

- company car
- holidays
- courses
- qualifications
- growth
- stock options
- bonus
- career counselling
- more authority – responsibility
- flexitime
- education
- project
- bigger computer
- bigger budget.

When a new salary is offered

You have three options:

1. Accept it, thanking the people verbally and in writing for their support of you.
2. Flinch gently and say, 'Oh, I was expecting a little more.'
3. Flinch significantly and say how disappointed you are.

Clearly, which one you choose, depends on your long-term strategy, your relationships and what your plans are.

Here are a few examples of soft flinches:

'I was expecting a little more than that.'

'Can you go to a bit more?'

'The market price seems to be a bit higher.'

'I have a family.'

'I have a mortgage to pay.'

'I was on £x five years ago; I was hoping for some more.'

Do not forget:

- *Update your CV regularly* – remind yourself what you are doing, the extras you are doing, what your qualifications are and what qualifications you are going to get next.

- *Update your LinkedIn profile regularly* – today, people are more likely to check your LinkedIn profile and other social media platforms that are in the public domain, either before they talk to you or before they think about offering you the job.

- *Keep your public profile professional* – it is better to be careful with what you put on sites like Facebook, as I have found that more than half of HR people check a candidate's Facebook account before they consider an interview.

- *Keep in touch with recruitment consultants (headhunters)* – the law of requisite variety says that the more options you have, the more advantage you will have. This is key in any type of negotiating, particularly salary negotiations. Talk to them, network with them, but make sure you stay in control; they are staffed with strong personalities who need to sell, and you are their product. Do not let them hassle you.

Hotspot 2
How to negotiate a discount

Mindset is key

You need the right mindset. The mindset to negotiate discounts at every opportunity. Frame this thought in your mind so that always you are thinking about how you can get money off.

You need to think you are going to get a reduced price on everything you buy from now. The results might surprise you. And, remember, everything you get a discount on is part of your tax-free disposable income that the revenue authorities cannot touch.

If you do not ask, you will not get

Negotiating a discount requires nothing more than asking. However, *how you ask* is key to the results you get.

Here are some other words/sentences you might use and say as a matter-of-fact statement:

'The usual discount, please.'

'The normal discount, please.'

If they say something like, 'Are you trade?', say, 'Yes – I always trade', and then make sure you smile.

Use the what who how method

> **T!P TOP TIP!**
> Once you get used to asking always, you will be surprised how often you succeed.

The what

First of all, look at what you believe to be the profitability of what you are buying – the margins the vendor is making.

If you think they are making a reasonable margin, then you should ask.

However, if you are buying food in a supermarket, I do not think you will get a discount easily. Here the discounts usually are given by way of loyalty cards, etc. Make sure you have all the loyalty cards you need and that you collect the points. The points often are worth more than you think, especially on certain days.

The who

Who should you ask for a discount? You should ask the manager or someone who looks like they have the authority to give a discount.

Go up to them and build rapport. Connect with them as we have talked about previously in the book. Create a little small talk. Then ask very nicely for a discount.

The how

How you do depends on the circumstances and you can do this in many ways. There is an element of judgement and intuition in this.

Here are some examples:

> 'If I buy this today, will you give me a discount?' The implication here is that you may not buy it.

> 'Do you have the authority to give discounts?' If they say yes, smile and say, 'Great! Could I have 15 per cent on this please?' If they say no, ask who does have the authority.

Voice tonality

Remember to use soft voice tonality.

If you ask tough questions, they are more acceptable if you ask them in a soft voice, lowering the volume, almost quietly so no one else can hear, even if there is no one within earshot.

If they say no to your request, do not give up

You might say, jokingly, 'I bet you could?' Watch their reaction to see if they might, and push more. If they say, definitely, no, then you either buy it and move on, or you see if you can get it elsewhere.

Go on? You could, couldn't you?

I was in the local branch of a well-known chain of stationers and I was buying files and papers that added up to £48.74. I asked if I could have the 'usual discount' as I do and the manager said 'We only give discounts to students.'

'That's OK,' I said, 'because I am a mature student.' He said, 'You will have to show me your student discount card.' I replied that I didn't have one, going on to say, 'However I study the highest achievers in the world and because I believe in life-long learning and practise it, that makes me a mature student.' He told me that didn't count and he'd have to see the evidence. I replied that I could get a 'mature student discount card' printed in an hour.

We were having a great laugh by this time and he then said, 'OK give me a break, you can have your discount' and pressed the discount button on the till.

I walked up the road, went into a digital printing shop and asked to have 1000 mature student discount cards printed.

An hour later I picked them up. I have included one below, please photocopy, write your name in and off you go.

Welcome to the Mature Students' Club. After all, you are reading this book which makes you a student of negotiation skills. Congratulations.

Mature Student Discount Card

- Normal Discount
- Best Offers
- Sharp Pricing

Do not forget:

- *Get into the negotiator's mindset* – always think about asking for a discount. Always expect to get a discount. If you cannot get a discount, ask for extras.

- *Practise how you ask* – the way you ask, gently or firmly, will be crucial to your success rate. People like giving things to people they like.

- *Always have other options* – if they think you might buy it elsewhere, then they know that, to get the sale, probably they have to come down to their walk away price.

- *Do not take a no as rejection* – it is just a discount that you have not got this time. Get over it, move on and ask for a discount on the next thing you buy.

- *Talk to other people who like getting discounts* – ask them what they do, how they do it, what they have obtained.

Hotspot 3
How to negotiate on the phone

Use the phone to your advantage

Speaking on the phone means you can engage in a two-way conversation where you can get an instant reaction to their proposals.

Build rapport in the usual way, a little small talk. Use the same words as the other person, if you can. For example, I answer the phone, 'Hello, it's Derek Arden.' You can play back two of the words I have used to build rapport, by saying, 'Hello, Derek. Is now a good time to speak or can I call you back?'

Do not miss the chance to connect with the other person, if you can. It will help the negotiation.

Make the call if you can

You can be better prepared if you make the outgoing call so that you are in the perfect frame of mind. Alternatively, arrange a time to speak so that, even if they are calling, you can still feel prepared.

If they call you and you were not expecting the call, then say it is not a convenient time for the call and arrange for a call back at a specific time. Alternatively, ask if you can call them back in a short time, giving you enough time to prepare yourself properly.

Be prepared

Make the environment conducive to your call. Close irrelevant programs on your computer. Put papers away. Go to a different room, or even walk outside.

Standing up whilst on the telephone gives you better body posture and, therefore, better concentration, with the mind body connection. You will also feel more confident and sharper, as there will be more oxygen flowing to your brain.

Get someone else to listen

If it is a difficult call or a complicated one, you could put the call on a speaker phone or you could have someone with a separate ear piece. (However, you should let the caller know that they are listening.)

The listener will be able to take notes and interpret the meaning while you are handling the negotiating. This can be really useful to revisit after the call.

Listen for what you cannot see

There is no body language to help us interpret the real meaning, so switch on your active listening skills. Focus on the call and the person at the other end of the call to listen for intention and any hesitations.

Take a break

Just as with all negotiations, if you need a break to think through your options, then agree to call the person back at a prearranged time, or send them an email in advance before you call them.

Do not forget:

- *Be polite, build rapport* – ask if this is a convenient time to have a conversation. Small talk is as important on the phone as it is face to face.

- *Use the person's name* – often, but not too often (too often can sound patronising and manipulative), mirror their language, the words, the tone and speed of voice.

- *Ask high-quality questions and listen carefully* – you will get clues to how it is going from the way they answer, as well as what they answer.

- *Summarise agreement* – listen carefully to whether they are in agreement by their tone of voice and language. Confirm agreement by email straight away. Write the contract.

Hotspot 4
How to negotiate as a team

Team negotiations usually get better results

Any functioning team tends to get increased performance, rather than operating solo. You have differing roles, differing views and you tend to notice different things.

Remember TEAM – together everybody achieves more.

Get someone else on your side

Any important negotiation needs more than one person to be involved. If it is not already the case and you can bring someone else onto your side, I would strongly advocate building a team, as it can be crucial to the success of your negotiating plans.

When you are directly involved in the negotiation bargaining process, it is very difficult to concentrate on what you are doing and, at the same time, take notes, observe the body language and sense what is happening.

If you do not have a team, then consider who you could ask. You could take a friend, a mentor, a colleague or someone you trust, as long as they have a clear brief on what their role is. Offer to reciprocate for them next time. You will be amazed what you learn in the observer's role.

Assign roles to team members

If you have the luxury of a larger team, then here are the roles of your dream team. Choose the number and the roles of your team carefully, and remember that briefing and debriefing is very important.

Lead negotiator (essential)

This is the person who leads the discussions, controls the silences and calls the timeouts. On most occasions this will be you, the reader. This is, generally, the most senior person or the person in charge. This is the pressure role where the focus of attention ends up. Often, this is the person with most at stake in the negotiation. This is why it can be important to the success of the negotiation that this person has help. The help can come in the form of a right-hand person, who can do some or most of the other roles, but particularly be the observer, the person who watches what is going on and what is happening.

Observer (essential)

This is a very active role, even though it appears to be passive from the other side's point of view. The observer must watch everything carefully: the body language, the nuances; listen to the actual words, how they are said and the tone and the feelings – what is said and what is not said and what might be left out deliberately.

The key time for team discussions will be during the time outs, breaks and adjournments. These, more often than not, you will have to call. Perhaps, like this – 'We have made a lot of progress. Would you mind if I had a couple of minutes with my team?'

Note taker (optional)

This is the recorder – the person who keeps the notes, the minutes. Also, they may write the agreement and the contract, or the record of what happened. If you do not have a note taker, then someone else in the team needs to keep clear records of everything said and agreed.

Expert (optional)

This can be the engineer, quantity surveyor, the technician, the product specialist, accountant or lawyer. Anyone you need there for his or her specialist knowledge.

They need to be briefed very diligently as to when they can speak. There is always a danger they might answer questions you pose to the other side. Sometimes, this can be a natural thing for them to do, as they want to show off their knowledge to the other side. Do not allow them to speak without coming through the leader of your team. They may have a close affinity to their opposite team member, which can be used to your advantage or to your detriment.

Interpreter (optional)

There are some long negotiations where you will need more than one interpreter. The cultural issues need to be carefully understood and you might need separate advice. Make sure the interpreter understands your goals and is briefed on when the important issues require silence.

Do not forget:

- *To have a team briefing* – this should cover the set-up of the team; who is going to say what and how. They need to understand that the team leader must always be in control.

- *Not to speak or answer any questions without permission (could be a nod, an exchange of eye contact, etc.) from the team leader* – this will ensure that the focus of the meeting, the strategy and the tactics are controlled. You do not want them speaking out of turn.

- *Take a time out* – the time out will give the team leader a break and enable the team members to put across their views, their ideas and to explain what they saw, heard and felt. This enables the team to move forward when the time out is over, towards the agreed outcome.

- *To have a team debriefing* – what went well, what you could do better next time, what they saw, heard and felt, how we operated as a team, how we are going to operate next time to be even better.

> **TIP TOP TIP!**
> When you learn you earn!

Hotspot 5
How to negotiate by email

Use emails to your advantage

Emails are useful when we are negotiating, if we are short of time, the amounts are insignificant and we do not need to see the other person's reaction. However, most other times, because it is one-way communication, with no immediate feedback, we should use it sparingly.

If you are not able to meet to discuss face to face, then email is a great alternative to keep the negotiation moving.

Email is also excellent for keeping records. Having a written record gives you an audit trail, so you can refer to previous exchanges.

Draft your email and review it carefully

Ask yourself if you have expressed yourself clearly, if you have answered their questions, and if there is any ambiguity.

If you are in any doubt about an email, there are a few precautions you should take. Address it to yourself so if there is any chance of a mistake it goes to you first and you can see what it looks like in your inbox.

1. Compose the email or reply in a new window, so it does not get sent by mistake before you are ready.

2. Do not press send too quickly. Print it out and read it through slowly. Whether you are starting a conversation or replying to an email, ensure that you have read through the email carefully to ensure it conveys what you want to say.

3. Leave it to the next morning, having slept on it, before you make the final decision. In the heat of the moment, you can be tempted to respond quickly, but, if things get tricky, often it pays to wait 24 hours before replying. It can also help to get a second opinion from someone you know and trust.

4. Do not forget that USING CAPITALS IN EMAIL IS JUST LIKE SHOUTING so do not do it. Using red is angry! And keep any bold

or italics to highlight occasional important points. Do not go overboard and format the whole email in bold and italic. However, remember that different email systems format in different ways. So, before delivery, your format might have been changed. Therefore, you might want to attach a PDF, if necessary.

Be business-like and friendly

Whilst emails should be business-like, never forget the human touch, as there is a person at the other end who wants to help. They are going to help the people who treat them courteously, with respect rather than abruptly or in an offhand way.

Round robin emails (copied to all) can lead to chaos and misunderstandings. It enables recipients to chip in and take no responsibility for their actions.

Isolate the recipients of emails by not replying to all. Initiate by sending direct, and personally without copying to all, if you think things may be contentious.

Clarify misunderstandings

If you think the other person has not understood what you meant, then address the issue directly and try to clarify what the problem is. Explain what you were saying a different way, or use imagery to help.

Remember that with email it can be hard to gauge tone, so ensure your language is appropriate.

Further, you will not be able to see their reaction so do not leave any room for confusion.

Email can be really useful when discussing specifics or finalising details. The great advantage is that you can see all the text of previous emails so, if you want to go back to something, you can copy and paste the relevant text.

Send at a good time

Psychologists have told me it can be the state or the frame of mind the recipient is in which determines how they interpret the email.

Additionally, the later in the day when people open emails might determine how favourably they receive it, together with the way they interpret key words in the email. The later in the afternoon or evening, the less favourably they may view it. Additionally they might read it late at night on their smart device and reply aggressively!

Do not forget:

- *Be polite* – always keep it friendly by including a personal note and asking how they are. Do not forget to use the recipient's name.

- *Keep it brief* – long emails tend not to be digested thoroughly, so keep it to the point, but not so short that it appears rude.

- *Give options* – make the email feel like an exchange, by offering options. Give them different packages, times, or locations, for example, 'If you can do . . . , we can do . . .'

- *Close courteously* – the habit of making emails with a time deadline on them and including no best wishes or 'Thanks for all your help' or something similar is not congruent to working towards a win win. Take five seconds longer to make it look better.

Hotspot 6
How to negotiate internationally

Overview

In this day and age we may need to negotiate internationally at some stage. This could be face to face, by phone, video conference, email or via the internet.

There are a number of factors we need to consider. These factors are culture, language, traditions, manners and goodwill. You have to get protocol and hierarchy right; some countries can be intolerant if you get it wrong.

However, now we negotiate in more of a global village with mass migration, *but* there are a number of stereotypes, so below are some guidelines.

As English almost is the universal language of business, it is important to realise that, whilst a person's English might be very good, they may be translating largely from their own language.

If it were possible, bringing in your local colleagues/agents/consultants to assist you could be a good move. It is always beneficial to show that you are connected in the country/jurisdiction, and that you are spreading economic benefit in the country as well.

Basic assumption

One of the basic assumptions of negotiating is that everyone is different in a variety of ways, so we need to understand the other side and where they are coming from.

This is even more important in international negotiations.

The golden rule

There is no golden rule!

Research the country you are going to before you go. Search the internet for customs, expectations, how the people respond, what they expect, how to dress and how to address the people you meet.

Talk to people who have been there. Ask via your social networks, social media and business colleagues.

Make no assumptions. Check and find out about the country, the people and the culture and the hierarchy of the organisation you are meeting.

Take the time to get the pronunciation of the names correct.

> **TIP TOP TIP!**
> No country is the same; no culture is the same.
>
> There are no rules; never make any assumptions.

Helpful guidelines

Here are some guidelines that you might find useful.

However, please do not take any of this as hard fact, as every circumstance will be different. These are generalisations. As with people, no two situations or people are the same.

Just for example, people who have travelled to the UK, Europe or the USA for their education, will have a more westernised approach than those who have never left their own country.

Europe

People are more likely to haggle the further south in Europe you go, just as time keeping also becomes less strict. Germans and Germanic culture is very punctual and efficient. Do not be late.

In some countries, negotiations can be really tough, even rude and aggressive, but, after the formalities have been agreed, the tone will be lighter and socialising will be expected. They might even expect you to be their friend at the end of the negotiation.

The Dutch might sound tough with their accents and could sound quite blunt in what they say, but they are not being rude; they are very polite people.

Scandinavians/Northern Europeans are not so forthcoming and play their cards close to their chests.

North America

In the USA they like to be tough with a no-nonsense approach. Get on with the negotiations quickly and do not give too much time to small talk. They like to be able to show colleagues that they have won.

One senior US negotiator told me that, in his experience, British people were more collaborative than Americans, who typically would be more aggressive in their negotiations.

In the USA, first names are used immediately.

An American client of mine, Tim Durkin, says,

> 'Americans can be all handshaking and back slapping and now even move to hugging, if the atmosphere is casual. However, they still recoil at the thought of touching each other in subways, buses or crowds. Americans would pass out, if they had to ride on a typical Tokyo train.'

South America/Latin America

Due to the mainly Southern European historical influences, often it is assumed that you can treat people from South America as if they are Spanish or Portuguese. However, whilst this is a reasonable rule of thumb, there are some real differences that it is worthwhile being aware of. There is also quite an Italian influence on some countries.

In Brazil, time is rarely an issue. In Argentina, people tend to be more punctual. Generally, in South America, hospitality is very important. Being able to converse in their language, particularly the initial greetings and general pleasantries, goes a long way to building rapport and being accepted.

This does, of course, apply everywhere. If you make a little effort, you will get a strong reward.

Middle East

Relationships are very important. The Arab culture is inherently warming and friendly but it takes time to build personal relationships. Time is not important to them.

However, they can have lots of advisers (expats from Europe, Asia or elsewhere in their region) and their negotiation style will reflect their original background with due recognition of their local cultural influences (their bosses).

As a rule, you should not shake hands with an Arab lady, if you are a man and vice versa.

Discounts on price with no reduction in scope are expected.

As I have said, Middle Eastern people tend to need time to build relationships, whereas some Western cultures, particularly the USA, like to get straight on with the business. In some places, great emphasis is placed on 'your word'.

Delicately, you might need to find out if the person you are negotiating with has the authority to negotiate and agree the deal. Referral 'back up the line' for final sanction is commonplace (overuse of higher authority).

I once heard of a Middle Eastern negotiation where the USA was heavily involved. They spent six months negotiating the size of the table and the food that was going to be served.

As an aside, and linked to the above, I was invited to do a talk in North Harrow. It turned out to be a scout hut that had been converted into a mosque. No one told me it was a sacred place and I walked in without taking my shoes off. I was politely and firmly put in my place.

Asia

On the Indian sub-continent they have been trading for many years across the seas and haggling hard is part of the negotiation process.

There is still an English influence in places like Hong Kong and Singapore, with a Chinese influence becoming stronger more recently.

Business cards should be treated as rare jewels – particularly in the Far East. You give them out two handed, accept them two handed and admire them.

Status is very important and this, for example, is reflected in the seating arrangements for meetings. The senior person sits away from the door and other attendees sit in order of seniority with the most junior nearest to the door (and, I am told, expected to fight off intruders!). This is the influence of Feng Shui on the region.

A Chinese contract was once described as a handshake; a commitment that was personal, and could not be broken. In today's litigious global world, that may not always be the case now *but* it tells us something about the culture.

I heard a story about a business group who went to Japan and tossed their business cards across the negotiating table. The Japanese were totally bemused by this potential Western insult.

Australia

The customs of Australia fit somewhere between the USA and the UK. Their sense of humour, like their negotiating, can be a bit abrasive or a bit quirky. For example, the Aussie way of talking about a friend, or even you, often can seem offensive to our ears. It is always a great idea to check whether an Australian is smiling when he says something that may at first be thought derogatory!

I checked into a hotel room in Melbourne, Australia and was given a room on the 42nd floor. When I asked to change it, however, they said they were full, in an unhelpful way. It was still in the early afternoon, so they could have swapped us round. I then said I did not like heights and they said, with a straight face, 'Well, don't look out the window, then.' This is an extreme example but, to me, did sum up some of the bluntness that I have met in Australia.

General hints

Nodding

In Japan nodding means 'I understand'; to Eskimos it means 'no'.

Touching

Touching is more acceptable in some cultures than others. In cultures and environments where touching is less common, the only safe place to make contact with someone, is around the elbow. A newspaper survey said that, in Milan, Italians sometimes touch each other 100 times a day. The same survey said that, in London, the Brits never touched, apart from the odd handshake.

A-OK

This is when the tips of the first finger and thumb are put together
in a circle.

- In the USA usually it means A-OK.
- In France usually it means zero.
- In Japan usually it means money.
- In Tunisia usually it means I will kill you.
- And, in a number of Eastern countries, it is seen as a very
  obscene gesture.

Thumbs up

The thumbs up gesture can mean agreed, everything is good, and it
can be a very rude gesture in some cultures. It is a positive gesture
in the West but, in the East, it can mean the opposite, so be careful.
I gave that signal to a Filipino once, without knowing, and he was
insulted. I had to apologise.

Soles of the feet

It is an insult to show the soles of your feet to another person.

In Libya, Colonel Gaddafi, the ruler of Libya, was seen to be showing
the soles of his feet to Tony Blair, the UK Prime Minister, when they
were negotiating the sanctions release and the issues about the
person who allegedly planted the Lockerbie bomb. Mr Blair seemed
oblivious to it but, as a politician in those circumstances, he had no
choice. No doubt his advisers would have told him afterwards that
there was not much chance of Gaddafi keeping to his word, as he
had posed for photographers with that gesture.

So, be careful whatever gestures you use – they may not cross
borders.

Cultural variances

I read that Stanford University researched, with Citigroup worldwide, this question:

> 'If one of your colleagues asked you to work on a big project, in what circumstances would you feel the most obligated to help?'

Here are the number-one reasons that came back:

- In Spain – if they knew my family or friends (liking/trust).
- In the Far East (Hong Kong) – if they knew my boss (authority).
- In the UK, the USA and Canada – if they had done something for me before (reciprocity).
- In Germany – if the rules of the company said I should (authority).

This shows that, internationally and culturally, we always need to understand that differences occur, quite substantial differences.

Note that there are many regional variations of body language and how people interact. It is very important that you check the differences with people who have intimate knowledge. You may need not just an interpreter but also a cultural interpreter.

For an international client coming to see someone in the UK, the more you can make their visit enjoyable, the more likely the negotiations will go smoothly:

- If you can, meet them at the airport. Alternatively, send a car for them, so they are met. Take them out to dinner. Show them around. Be a great host.
- Afford them a few minutes with the most senior person in the office. They may see this as a privilege, even if that person is not involved in the negotiation. 'Let me introduce you to our Chairman . . .'

Do not forget:

- Time is important to cultures – in some cultures, like Germany, if you are not punctual, the negotiation could be cancelled. In the Middle East, time is not an issue; I have heard of negotiations that started an hour late. I was sent to coach a sheikh in the Royal Palace in Abu Dhabi. It was a two-day programme; he turned up one hour late each day. That was normal I was later told.

- *The ambiance/the set-up* – what time the meeting will take place and where. Do you need to take any small gifts, tokens of appreciation? How will the seating be? How many people will they have on their side? How many do you need?

- *Put yourself in the other side's shoes* – what are their objectives? What are their goals? What can we do to be more like them? Remember, people are influenced by people they like. This is the PLM factor: people like me.

- *Do not take strange things personally* – it may be something cultural. Remember, you will be out of your comfort zone overseas, so it may be you over-reacting to something that has happened and that they find normal.

- *The golden rule* – there is no golden rule. But there are guidelines that need to be thought about.

The solution to the 9 dots puzzle in Chapter 5:

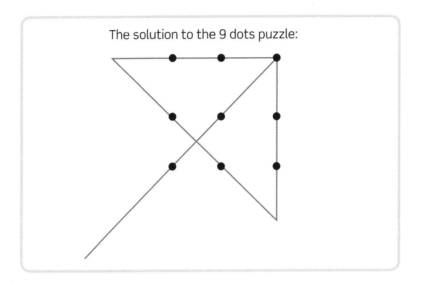

The solution to the 9 dots puzzle:

Often the solution is outside the box.

Other titles by Derek Arden

Everything is negotiable, DVD/CD set

Presenting phenomenally – How to succeed at presenting (2008),
Tiptree House Publishing

*The 97 secret tips that the top negotiators don't want you to
know!*, CD Audiobook (2006), Tiptree House Publishing

Negotiating success – Live inspirational talk at Surrey University
Business School – CD

The secret language of success – Understanding body talk

117 handy haggling hints – How to negotiate win win win deals,
with Peter Thomson, (2006), Tiptree House Publishing

DEREK ARDEN LIVE

As one of the top Professional Negotiation Speakers in the world, Derek is available to speak at your convention or run a masterclass to help you and your business make more money

Derek is also available to comment on a range of topics, including current topical negotiations, haggling situations and reading body language.

He has been featured on ITV, Meridian, BBC Radio 2 and Radio 4, Radio London, the *Financial Times*, the *Daily Mail* and many TV and radio stations in this country and the many other countries where he works.

Derek can advise clients on their negotiating strategy, tactics and moves; helping them make more money, get more business and have more confidence.

If you would like to get in touch, please contact the Derek Arden team:

Telephone **08450 574116** or **+44 7980 241185**
Email **action@derekarden.co.uk**
Visit **www.derekarden.com**

Index